THE SAT WORD SLAM

RHYME YOUR WAY TO A BETTER VOCABULARY
AND HIGHER SAT AND ACT SCORES

JODI FODOR. MFA

Aadamsmedia

AVON, MASSACHUSETTS

Published by
Adams Media, a division of F+W Media, Inc.
57 Littlefield Street, Avon, MA 02322. U.S.A.
www.adamsmedia.com

ISBN 10: 1-60550-025-9
ISBN 13: 978-1-60550-025-6

Printed in the United States of America.

J I H G F E D C B A

Library of Congress Cataloging-in-Publication Data
is available from the publisher.

This publication is designed to provide accurate and authoritative information with
regard to the subject matter covered. It is sold with the understanding that the
publisher is not engaged in rendering legal, accounting, or other professional advice.
If legal advice or other expert assistance is required, the services of a competent
professional person should be sought.
   —From a *Declaration of Principles* jointly adopted by a Committee of the
American Bar Association and a Committee of Publishers and Associations

Many of the designations used by manufacturers and sellers to distinguish their
products are claimed as trademarks. Where those designations appear in this book
and Adams Media was aware of a trademark claim, the designations have been
printed with initial capital letters.

This book is available at quantity discounts for bulk purchases.
For information, please call 1-800-289-0963.

This book is for Erin O'Connell
who taught me playfulishness with wordisms.

Thanks, Mom.

Acknowledgments

I happily thank my delightful students who helped me create and polish the rhymes and the mnemonics. Thank you very much for the effort and for all the laughs: Jake, Molly, Matthew, Hayley, Jenna, Michihito, Mamika, Sarah, Dylan, Kyle, Paige, Chase, Lindsey, Stephanie, Haley, Kristen, Chih, Rylan, Tyler, Alison, Griffin, and Lindsay.

Thanks to the team at Adams Media, especially Paula Munier, Wendy Simard, and Matthew Glazer for your vision, support, and professionalism.

I thank my dear friend and fellow writer, Tom Towles, who pushed and cheered me to "Write the thing!" and who introduced me to my wonderful agent.

The greatest thanks to the agent herself, Katharine Sands of the Sarah Jane Freymann Literary Agency, whose infinite enthusiasm and support was and is an inspiration.

Using This Book

Hey, read this part.
It's **short**!
It helps.

The *SAT Word Slam* will give you a very strong grasp of the meanings of 517 SAT-type words. This book doesn't try to shove dictionary-style definitions down your throat; instead, it presents the words within smart-aleck rhymes. That makes the thing a boatload more fun to read than the dictionary. Read these rhymes enough times and you'll be able to use all 517 words in your speech and writing, and you'll understand them when you hear or see them out in the wild.

As I'm sure you know by now, if you have a broad vocabulary, college entrance exams are going to be a lot more fun for you. Otherwise, you're in big trouble. For example, the sentence completions part of the SAT is essentially one big vocabulary test.

Pay attention to the **words in bold print.** They offer you shades of the featured word's meaning.

The first 339 words are presented in individual "poems" of their own, and the other 178 words are listed in "root families." Some knowledge of Greek and Latin roots will help you to dissect many words on the fly. For example, if you know that "mal" is bad, you can take a more educated guess about words that start with that prefix. If you see "malfeasance" on the SAT or ACT, you might not know its definition, but you can guess that whatever it is, it ain't good. Sometimes a sense of whether a word is positive or negative is enough to save your hide on these exams.

1. Read each word out loud a few times (the pronunciation is right there for you). The syllable in all CAPS is the one you should EM-fuh-size.

Erudite
(adj) "AIR-yoo-dite"

2. Read each rhyme several times and let the rhythm of it get into your mind, like song lyrics that stay with you. Re-reading these things is going to be a big part of making the clues stick.

3. Repeat each "**REMEMBER THIS**" clue a few times—think about it—and you'll start to cement the word into your memory. In every case, the "Remember This" is intended to leave you with something logical, something catchy, something that rhymes—some kind of mnemonic device to help you remember the meaning of the word long after you close this book.

4. Finally, you'll see "**Now you:**" after each word. This is a space for you to write memory clues that have to do with your own life and knowledge. For example, I can always remember that "gregarious" means "friendly and outgoing" because my brother **Greg** is **gregarious**. If you knew my brother Greg, I would have put that clue in the book!

Whenever you can think of a clue that's specific to your life, your opinions, your friends, your experience, and so on, **write it on the "Now you" line. The personal clues will be VERY helpful.**

Pronunciation Guide:
A=short "a" like "St**a**nd b**a**ck 'cause you **a**ct wh**a**cked."
OE=long "o" as in "G**o** h**o**me, you h**o**peless d**o**pe."
O or **OH**=short "o" as in "St**o**p c**a**lling yo mama."
EH=short "e" as in "That F**e**ndi dr**e**ss would look b**e**tter on an **e**lephant."
I or **IH**=short "i" as in "W**i**mpy s**i**ssies h**i**t their s**i**sters."
G=hard "g" as in "**G**et your **g**um off my **g**reat-**g**randma's **g**rave."
ZH=the "sio" part of "Use preci**sio**n on that brain inci**sio**n."

The rest of them are pretty obvious.

Remember (and this is very important): when you learn the words in this book and then go kick the crap out of the college entrance exams, you're going to make me look good, so get to it.

I hope you enjoy reading these rhymes as much as I enjoyed writing them. Imagine a job that keeps you giggling all day.

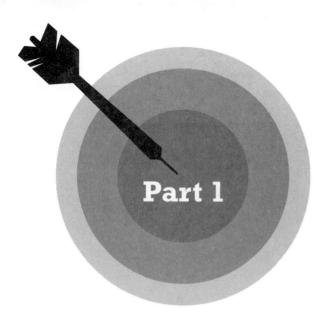

Part 1

The Individual Words

You ready? Let's get started. . .
Get your butt on the train.
I'm using rhyme and humor
To enlighten your brain.

So pay attention
To the definitions (**in bold**),
And memorize each word's "Remember This"

Then you're gold.

Abase

(verb) "Uh-BASE"

To **embarrass** or to **humble**,
To **make one a disgrace**.
Barry Bonds was **blushing**
When he couldn't steal *a base*.

*A base*ball player was *abased* when he couldn't steal *a base*.

Now you:

_____

_____

_____

_____

_____

Abhor

(verb) "Ab-HOR"

Abhor means to **hate**.
So simple it's great.

I abhor eating liver.
I **abhor** cigarettes.
I **abhor** crappy drivers
Who make nasty threats.

Here comes a clue,
Kinda simple and groovy:
Because I **hate** blood,
I **abhor** horror movies.

I ab*hor horror* movies.

Now you:

_____

_____

_____

_____

_____

Abrogate

(verb) "AB-roe-gate"

It means to **do away with**,
Eliminate, dispose.
If you don't want to wash the car,
Abrogate the hose.

Abrogate your enemies.
Abrogate your debt.
If your boyfriend is a jerk,
Abrogate his red Corvette.

REMEMBER THIS:

Abrogate=eliminate.

Now you:

_____
_____
_____
_____
_____

Acolyte

(noun) "AK-oe-lite"

An **acolyte worships**.
He **follows the code**.
He might **help at his church**
If that job's been bestowed.
If he knocks on your door,
He is there to invite:
"Come and join us, my brotha,
'Cause I've _seen the light_!"

REMEMBER THIS:

An aco*lyte* has seen the *light*.

Now you:

_____
_____
_____
_____
_____

Acquiesce

(verb) "Ak-wee-ESS"

Do you always **give in**?
Then you **acquiesce**.
You **never say no**;
It's just **yes—yes—yes**.

Careful with that—
Don't become a door mat.
Acquiescing is fine
But not all the time.

REMEMBER THIS:

To acqu*iesce* is to say *yes*.

Now you:

_____

_____

_____

_____

_____

Acumen

(noun) "AK-yoo-men"

When you behave with **acumen**,
You're **smart** with **keen insight**,
Like when you make
Shrewd business deals
Or stay out of a fight.
I know funny men and happy men,
Never men, forever men,
Gentle men, and wacky men,
But where are all the **acu-men**?

REMEMBER THIS:

Show me the smart acu-men!

Now you:

_____

_____

_____

_____

_____

Adulterate

(verb) "Uh-DUL-ter-ate"

To **make something cheaper**,
To **make it impure**.
This word isn't nice to adults,
That's for sure.

Willy Wonka liked kids
But adults—not so much
'Cause he saw them **adulterate**
Much that they touch.

Adults have *adult*erated the environment.

Now you:

_____
_____
_____
_____
_____

Aggrandize

(verb) "Uh-GRAN-dize"

To **widen in scope**, to **increase in size**,
Make greater in power—
That's **aggrandize**.

You know what I hate when I listen to rap?
It's that me . . . me . . . me . . . me
Self-**aggrandizing** crap.
If you talk yourself up,
Like you're all big and sure,
The fact is you're probably way insecure.
Try **aggrandizing** everyone else . . .
Trust me here.
You're bound to be voted
Best Friend of the Year.

To ag*grand*ize is to make more *grand*.

Now you:

_____
_____
_____
_____
_____

Ambiguous

(adj) "Am-BIG-yoo-us"

If you're being **ambiguous**
I **don't know what you mean**.
Your answers aren't firm,
So which way do you lean?

Ambi means **both** or **two**.
Do you understand?
An **ambi**dextrous artist
Can draw with **both** hands.

Ambiguous statements
Are annoyingly **vague**,
Like: "*You may or may not
Have contracted the plague!*"

Ambi=two, both.

Now you:

_____

Ameliorate

(verb) "Uh-MEEL-yor-ate"

This means to **makes things better**,
To **improve a situation**.
Let's **ameliorate** our glumness
With a big fat Greek vacation.

I'm not much into cooking,
But I can give this advice:
You'll **ameliorate** your meals
The day you learn to add some spice.

Spices can a*meli*orate *meals*.

Now you:

_____

Anomaly

(noun) "Uh-NOM-uh-lee"

An **anomaly** is something that's
Out of the norm.
It's just an **abnormal condition**.
Like a dark-headed kid
From a family of blondes.
That might cause a little suspicion.

REMEMBER THIS:

An a-nomaly is a-normal.

Now you:

_____

_____

_____

_____

_____

Antipodal

(adj) "An-TIP-uh-dul"

Antipodal things are just **opposites**.
Up and down, in and out, wrong and right.
Now help me with these two expressions
That seem to be having a fight:
"I'm up for that" and
"I'm down with that" . . .
These expressions are saying the same,
But don't they sound pretty **antipodal**?
Alas, it's the young language game.

REMEMBER THIS:

Anti=opposed.
An*tip*odal things *tip* in opposite directions.

Now you:

_____

_____

_____

_____

_____

Antithesis

(noun) "An-TITH-ih-sis"

It's the **opposite point**.
A **contradictory position**.
That's about it. That's the whole definition.
Think of a thesis—it's your point of view.
Anti*t*hetic people
Will just **argue** with you.

Antithesis is against your opinion, or "anti" your thesis.

Now you:

_____

_____

_____

_____

_____

Apathy

(noun) "AP-uh-thee"

Apathy means that you **just don't care**.
You can't get your big **lazy**
Butt off the chair.
You don't want to vote,
You don't want to write,
Don't want to wake up
After sleeping all night.

Because of *apathy* I don't give a *crapathy*.

Now you:

_____

_____

_____

_____

_____

Apparition

(noun) "Ap-uh-RISH-un"

An **apparition just appears**,
Some kind of **ghost** or **phantom spirit**.
It's something you can **see**,
But more than likely you can't hear it
(And I'll bet you kind of fear it).

An *appa*rition *app*ears.

Now you:

_____

_____

_____

_____

_____

Arbitrary

(adj) "AR-bih-trare-ee"

It's an **unexplainable** choice
Based on who knows what?
Make **arbitrary** decisions,
And you're called a **random** nut.

I wanted a really nice dinner
And invited my nutty friend Larry.
He said, "Let's walk up to Arby's."
That's what I call **arbitrary**.

He made an *arb*itrary decision to go to *Arb*y's.

Now you:

_____

_____

_____

_____

_____

Arboreal

(adj) "Ar-BOR-ee-ul"

Arboreal means **pertaining to trees**.
Arboreal structures sway in the breeze.
Arbors give shade,
And they make the air clean.
Be good to the **arbors**—
We need to be green.
You know what I mean?

Arboreal *trees* sway in the *breeze*.

Now you:

_____

_____

_____

_____

_____

Arcane

(adj) "Ar-KANE"

Something **arcane** is **mysterious**;
It's **not easily understood**.
It's **cryptic**, which means kind of **secret**,
Like a language unique to your hood.

So here's something I find **arcane**:
It's hanging out in an arcade
And dumping your precious allowance
Until every game has been played.

Going to the *arca*de is *arca*ne (to me, anyway).

Now you:

_____

_____

_____

_____

_____

Ascetic

(noun) "Uh-SET-ik"

This kind of person lives
A **lean** and **modest life**.
No Porsches or Ferraris,
No diamonds for the wife.
No indulgences, **no waste**—
It's a **simple** kind of taste.

Old Donald Trump—
    he's a big money guy—
He might see an **ascetic** monk
    and then cry:
"Your life is **ascetic**.
    Oh Man, that's pathetic."
Greedy The Donald is unsympathetic
(On top of that he's unkindly poetic).

REMEMBER THIS:

*Ascet*ics don't have many *assets* (not financial ones, anyway).

Now you:

_____

_____

_____

_____

_____

Asinine

(adj) "ASS-ih-nine"

Asinine is **stupid** and **silly** and **dumb**.
You would look **asinine**
Sucking your thumb.
The very best feature that **asinine**'s got
Is it sounds like you're swearing
When really you're not.

REMEMBER THIS:

Asinine=making an *ss of yourself.

Now you:

_____

_____

_____

_____

_____

Assiduous

(adj) "Uh-SID-yoo-us"

If you are **assiduous**
You **work really hard**.
You could be cramming for a test
Or simply cleaning the yard.

Assiduous: working your *ss off.

Now you:

_____

_____

_____

_____

_____

Astute

(adj) "Uh-STOOT"

Astute people are **clever** and **wise**.
Listen up girls, I want to advise:
Skip the bad boys and date **astute** guys.
In the long run, believe me,
Astute is the prize.

If you're astute, you're not astupid.

(*Say that one like an Italian. And talk with your hands while you're at it.*)

Now you:

_____

_____

_____

_____

_____

Audacious

(adj) "Aw-DAY-shus"

Do you want to be a movie star?
You'd better be **audacious**.
Extremely bold and **fearless**
And **persistent** (that's **tenacious**).
'Cause movie stars and other entertainers
Like musicians
Must learn to be **audacious**
Just to make it through auditions.

REMEMBER THIS:

You need to be *aud*acious to survive *aud*itions.

Now you:

_____

_____

_____

_____

_____

A

August

(adj) "Aw-GUST"

I can't tell you how much I love New York.
I wish I could eat the whole place
With a fork.
When you feel **admiration**
This **grand** and **robust**
That is to say that your view is **august**.

If you're treated **augustly**
You're rich, like the queen.
Central Park in late August . . .
Awww, that's what I mean.

REMEMBER THIS:

Think "Aw, gush."
I *gush* about things that are au*gust*.

Now you:

_____

_____

_____

_____

_____

Auspicious

(adj) "Aw-SPISH-us"

Auspicious things are **favorable**;
It's all looking good.
Do you accept **auspicious** offers?
Believe me, you should.
Oscar night is **awesome**;
You might say that it's **auspicious**—
A night that **can fulfill**
An actor's loftiest **wishes**.

*Aus*picious is *awes*ome.

Now you:

_____

_____

_____

_____

_____

Austere

(adj) "Aw-STEER"

Serious and **moral.**
Very strict is **austere.**
It sounds like those Catholic school nuns
    that kids fear.
She's **trying to keep you in line**,
So a nun
Will steer toward **austere**
And away from the fun.

A nun will *steer* you to be au*stere*.

Now you:

_____

_____

_____

_____

_____

Bacchanal

(noun) "BAK-uh-nol"

A **bacchanal**: this is a **drunken fiesta**,
A **party**,
A **loud celebration**.
It was named after Bacchus, the great god
of wine . . .
Named also for **intoxication**.

There sure seem to be quite a few
bacchanals
In LA
And who's paying the tab
For all these young stars getting famous
in bars
And landing their butts in rehab?

Too many *bacch*anals will send you *back* to
rehab.

Now you:

_____

_____

_____

_____

_____

B

Banal

(adj) "Buh-NOL"

Banal writers will **bore** you silly.
Their work is just **common**
And **stale**—
I mean, *really*.
They use **old expressions**
You hear every day.
When someone's **banal**,
He is **trite** and **cliché**.
As your new writing teacher
I must take a stand:
All **banal** writing from now on is banned.

Let's *ban all banal* writing.

Now you:

_____

_____

_____

_____

_____

Bantam

(adj) "BAN-tum"

Little, **short**, **tiny**—there you have
   bantam.
It also means **feisty** and **small**.
A **bantam**weight boxer
   can't weigh very much,
So I'm guessing he's also **not tall**.

Jack Russell puppies and
   Baby doll dishes . . .
Bantam describes many things,
Like munchkins in Oz and aquarium fishes
Or hobbits in *Lord of the Rings*.

REMEMBER THIS:

Bantam=small, like a bantamweight boxer.

Now you:

_____

_____

_____

_____

_____

Beget

(verb) "Bee-GET"

To **cause**, **produce**, or **generate**.
Those words define **beget**.
You can grasp the concept
Without breaking a sweat.
Violence **begets** more violence.
Love **begets** more love.
Fear **begets** more fear.
Do you get what I'm speaking of?

REMEMBER THIS:

You'll be gettin what you'll be begettin.
(*I'll be getting it for that one.*)

Now you:

_____

_____

_____

_____

_____

Benevolent

(adj) "Ben-EV-oe-lent"

Benevolent people are **sweet**
And they're **kind**.
If you live in the country
They're easy to find.
They're **generous** people
Who **donate a lot**.
If you're not **benevolent** I wonder why not.

The **bene** is from Latin for **positive**, **good**.
Have you learned any Latin?
Get on it—you should.

REMEMBER THIS:

*Bene*volent people *bene*fit others.

Now you:

_____
_____
_____
_____
_____

B

Benign

(adj) "Beh-NINE"

Benign is **harmless**.
Benign is **mild**.
As a child were you **benign** or wild?

If the doctor tells you,
"The test showed **benign**,"
Go have a party.
You're going to be **fine**.

REMEMBER THIS:

Benign is just fine.

Now you:

_____
_____
_____
_____
_____

Bent

(noun) "BENT"

Bent is in this book?
What's up with that?
You've known the meaning of the word
Since you were just a brat.

This one is a different **bent**.
This word is a noun.
It's a **natural inclination**
Or **an interest** you've found.

Ms. Aguilera's singing:
Now there you have a **bent**.
She's kinda tacky, but her voice
Was surely **heaven sent**.

You *bend* in the direction of your *bent*.

Now you:

_____

_____

_____

_____

_____

Berate

(verb) "Bee-RATE"

Jerks **criticize** and **yell** at you?
Berate them back.
Try hitting, too.

My work was rated
Only "B,"
So Dad and Mom **berated** me.

My report card was "*B*" *rated*, so I was *berated*.

Now you:

_____

_____

_____

_____

_____

Bigamist

(noun) "BIG-uh-mist"

A bigamist is someone with two different spouses.
This guy had better buy **two** roomy houses.
I've heard men complain about **wives**,
Haven't you?
So what kind of goofball
Would hook up with **two**?

A *big*amist needs a *big* house.

Now you:

_____

_____

_____

_____

_____

B

Blasé

(adj) "Bloh-ZAY"

It's bored with life and unimpressed.
You yawn despite a lot of rest.
I'm high on life, so I can say
I never waste my time **blasé**.

The **blasé** guy was tired of work.
The money was bad, his boss was a jerk.
So he finally quit.
What a great day:
He took charge of his life
And stopped being **blasé**.

*Bla*sé is kind of *blah*.

Now you:

_____

_____

_____

_____

_____

Bombastic

(adj) "Bom-BASS-tik"

I'll bet you know **bombastic** guys.
They **think they're all that**
And a bucket of fries.
They **strut** round the room
Like they're peacocks in bloom,
But they're just little boys in disguise.

A *bomb*astic guy thinks he's the *bomb*.

Now you:

_____

_____

_____

_____

_____

Boorish

(adj) "BOOR-ish"

Boorish people are just plain **rude**.
They're experts in **bad attitude**.
Boorish girls think they're so clever,
They flip their hair and say "*Whatever.*"

*Bor*at is pretty *boor*ish.

Now you:

_____

_____

_____

_____

Brevity

(noun) "BREV-ih-tee"

With **brevity** you're **brief**.
You say it **in no time flat**.
So in the spirit of **brevity**,
I won't say any more about that.

REMEMBER THIS:

*Br*evity=*br*ief.

Now you:

_____

_____

_____

_____

_____

Bromidic

(adj) "Broe-MID-ik"

A **bromidic** expression is **worn out**.
It's **trite**, it's **cliché**, and it's **stale**.
"Amazing," is one that's **bromidic**.
When I hear it I just want to wail.
"That salad's amazing!"
"Your hair is amazing!"
This is the nonsense I hear.
What would be truly amazing
Is world peace or a three-headed deer.

Americans say lots of **bromides**,
But that is the worst one I know.
Oh yeah, here's another that's dopey:
To greet *every* guy with "Hey, Bro."

REMEMBER THIS:

Calling *everyone* "bro" is bromidic.

Now you:

_____

_____

_____

_____

_____

Bumptious

(adj) "BUMP-shus"

Pushy, forward, cocky, brash.
Bumptious people
Will sift through your trash.
Or they'll bump you right out of
The Coffee Bean line,
And when your drink's ready, they yell,
"Hey! That's mine!"

*Bump*tious people will *bump* you out of line.

Now you:

_____

_____

_____

_____

_____

Burgeon

(verb) "BUR-jin"

Developing, growing
Like flowers in spring . . .
Teenagers blush
When they start **burgeoning**.

Judd Apatow writes hilariously,
And his movie career sure did **burgeon**
With films like *Pineapple Express*, *Superbad*,
And the one with the really old virgin.

The 40-Year-Old Virgin helped Judd *burgeon*.

Now you:

_____

_____

_____

_____

_____

Cache

(noun) "KASH"

A **cache** is a name for a **hiding place**,
A **place to put all your best treasure**.
If you find your big sister's
Covert, hidden cache
Her journals should give you great pleasure.

Indiana Jones would whip and slash
Nazis and snakes
On his way to a **cache**.

Stash your *cash* in a secretive *cache*.

Now you:

_____

_____

_____

_____

_____

Cacophony

(noun) "Kuh-KOF-uh-nee"

This is a word that means
Nasty, harsh sounds.
Like the **discordant** music
Upon which Dad frowns.

When I was into heavy metal,
Grunge and raging punk
My father called my music
"A **cacophony** of junk."

Ca*coph*ony—sounds about as pleasant
as a *cough*.

Now you:

_____

_____

_____

_____

_____

Cadaver

(noun) "Kuh-DAV-er"

It's a **corpse**. It's a **dead body**.
It's a **person when he's dead**.
My brother grabbed my birthday Barbie
Then ripped off her head.
He handed her to me and laughed,
"Ha ha! She's a **cadaver**."
So I shoved her in the cake and said,
"Happy Birthday. You can have her."

REMEMBER THIS:

Barbie the *cadaver*—you can *have her*.

Now you:

_____

_____

_____

_____

_____

Cajole

(verb) "Kuh-JOLE"

You're **trying to get your own way**,
Nothing less
By **flattering** someone and **talking B.S**.
Cajoling is "**B.S. ing**."
I can't spell it out.
Your parents aren't too big on swearing,
No doubt.

REMEMBER THIS:

To get the lead *role*: *Cajole! Cajole!*

Now you:

_____

_____

_____

_____

_____

Calumnious

(adj) "Kuh-LUM-nee-us"

Calumnious people say
Scandalous things.
They **trash reputations**.
They write it, it stings.
"Brad!"
"Angelina!"
"Prince Will!
"The Queen Mother!"
Every **gossip** writer
Seems as stupid as another.

Gossip *column*s are *calumn*ious.

Now you:

_____

_____

_____

_____

_____

Cantankerous

(adj) "Kan-TANK-er-us"

Let's look back to the past
To good old Sesame Street
Where the **Grouch** in the trash can
Was **not pleasant or sweet**.
So yes, he was **cantankerous**;
With **nothing nice to say**,
But like many **grumpy** TV guys
We liked him anyway.

Can*tankerous* is really *crankerous*.

(*I* know *that was bad. You don't need to tell me when they're bad.*)

Now you:

_____

_____

_____

_____

_____

Capacious

(adj) "Kuh-PAY-shus"

Capacious is the easiest rhyme
Of my entire mission
'Cause **capacious** rhymes with **spacious**,
And **spacious** is the definition.

Capacious means *spacious*.

Now you:

_____

_____

_____

_____

_____

Capitulate

(verb) "Kuh-PICH-oo-late"

It means to **give up**,
To **throw in the towel**,
Surrender,
To **call it a day**.
In the War of U.S. Independence
We pushed all those Redcoats away.
They finally **gave up**.
Yeah, they **pitched in the towel**.
After eight years of trying to scare us,
They cried, "Hang on, Mate!
We will **capitulate**!"
Then we all signed the Treaty of Paris.

To ca*pit*ulate is to *pitch* in the towel.

Now you:

_____

_____

_____

_____

_____

Capricious

(adj) "Kuh-PREE-shus"

Capricious means **unpredictable**
Which can be kind of fun,
Like when my **capricious**
Health-freak mom
Bought a case of Capri Sun.

Mom *capri*ciously bought *Capri* Sun.

Now you:

_____

_____

_____

_____

_____

Captious

(adj) "KAP-shus"

Captious people **find fault in others**.
I feel bad for people
With **captious** mothers.
They **nitpick** and **judge**,
And you **simply can't please** 'em.
The best you can hope
Is to vaguely appease 'em.

So here comes your clue:
Think political cartoons.
Where elected officials
Look like old buffoons.
I love the sarcasm, I love the dark wit,
So for me, **captious** captions
And cartoons are *it*.

Political cartoon *captions* are *captious*.

Now you:

_____

_____

_____

_____

_____

Catatonic

(adj) "Kat-uh-TON-ik"

Think of a cat stretching out in the sun,
Like a **zombie** cat, **mellow** and **dazed**.
When my cat is like that,
All alone in the zone,
Even fireworks leave her **unfazed**.

Catatonic pretty much means **zoned out**
And **staring way off into space**.
But **catatonia** can switch you to **hyper**
With the look of a **spaz** on your face.

REMEMBER THIS:

*Cata*tonic: think of how a *cat* acts:
    sometimes zonked out and sometimes spazzy.

Now you:

_____

_____

_____

_____

Celerity

(noun) "Sell-AIR-ih-tee"

This word means **quickness**, **swiftness**.
It means **with racing speed**.
I'll link the word to celery
If I can find the link I need . . .
Oh, I hate that stringy vegetable,
So I used to eat it last.
Now I eat celery with **celerity**
To get rid of it **fast**.

REMEMBER THIS:

Eat *celer*y with *celer*ity.

Now you:

_____

_____

_____

_____

_____

Chagrined

(adj) "Shuh-GRINNED"

It's **embarrassed** and **ashamed**.
You'd be **chagrined**, I do suppose
If you laughed while drinking Starbucks
And the foam flew out your nose.

When you're cha*grin*ed, just *grin*.

Now you:

_____

_____

_____

_____

_____

Chastise

(verb) "CHAS-tize"

Do you know any people
Who **berate** and **criticize**?
These are folks who feel the need
To **punish** and **chastise**:
"You always date the wrong kind of guys!"
"Stop eating fries; you're getting fat thighs!"

Listen to me if you're wise:
Choose friends who advise;
Dump the ones who **chastise**.

To chastise is to criticize.

Now you:

_____

_____

_____

_____

Clamor

(noun) "KLAM-er"

Clamor is **an outburst** of
Loud, annoying noise.
Just like on a playground
Where the girls are chasing boys.

A house construction on my street
Has caused a lot of **clamor**.
All day long I hear
A dozen stinking, **banging** hammers.

Clamor—like the banging of a hammer.

Now you:

_____

_____

_____

_____

_____

Clandestine

(adj) "Klan-DES-tin"

It's **sneaky** and it's **hidden**.
It's **something undercover**.
She planned **clandestine** meetings
With her new, forbidden lover.

Klan members are **clandestine**
As they **hide** beneath their hoods.
That's because they're cowards,
Doing nothing any good.

Klan members are *clan*destine.

Now you:

_____

_____

_____

_____

_____

Coddle

(verb) "KOH-dul"

It's to **treat someone gently**—
Indulge him and **baby** him.
You "let" him and "give" him
And "yes" him and "maybe" him.

My grandma would plead to my mother,
"Don't **coddle** her.
You'll only end up with
A big teenaged toddler!"

A toddler wants you to cuddle her and
coddle her.

Now you:

_____

_____

_____

_____

_____

Coerce

(verb) "Koe-ERSE"

Were you **harshly persuaded**?
Then you were **coerced**.
Being **pushed into something**—
My friend, that's the worst.
My girlfriend **coerced** me
To ride on Space Mountain,
And man, was she sorry . . .
I barfed like a fountain.

Being coerced is the worst.

Now you:

_____

_____

_____

_____

Complacent
(adj) "Kum-PLAY-sent"

When you are **complacent**,
You **don't work hard** for more.
You're **happy with**
The level of achievement
Earned before.

You're **cozy** and **self-satisfied**;
Your work is **good enough**.
Be **complacent** in the gym
And chicks will never call you buff.

If you're com*place*nt you're kind of stuck in one *place*.

Now you:

_____

_____

_____

_____

_____

Compunction
(noun) "Kum-PUNK-shun"

Did you ever see
The very funny movie: ***Perfect Score***?
The kids want SAT scores
Over those they earned before.
They scheme to steal the SAT
And plan this big crusade.
They end up with the answers,
And they think they've got it made.
But in the end their **sense of shame**
Protects them from deceit.
Compunction equals **conscience** and
Won't let those people cheat.

Your sense of com*punc*tion won't let you be a *punk*.

Now you:

_____

_____

_____

_____

_____

Conducive

(adj) "Kun-DOO-siv"

Conducive means
Helpful toward reaching a goal.
Pit bulls are **conducive** to
Good crowd control.
If you plan to sneak food into class
Bring what's **handy**.
It's just not **conducive**
To pack cotton candy.

So here's a quick memory trick:
Think "**can do**."
If something's **conducive**,
It's **useful** to you.

REMEMBER THIS:

With something *condu*cive you *can do* things
more easily.

Now you:

_____

_____

_____

_____

_____

Conundrum

(noun) "Kuh-NUN-drum"

A **conundrum** is kind of a **problem**,
A **dilemma** or maybe a **puzzle**.
The chatty-mouth-sister **conundrum**
Was solved
When I bought her a sister-sized muzzle.

So picture a band
Where they all play guitar
(This clue's kind of silly and dumb);
The band's incomplete
'Cause they don't have a beat;
The **conundrum** is none of them drum.

REMEMBER THIS:

In his band, none can drum. That's a conundrum.

Now you:

_____

_____

_____

_____

_____

Covert

(adj) "KOE-vert"

It's an **under-cover**, **well-disguised**,
Or **secret operation**.
I was **covert** at sixteen
While following temptation.
My crew **sneaked** out
Our bedroom windows
(Some at crazy heights),
We crashed a party,
Then we slithered back before the light.
We were pretty clever **sneaks**,
Clandestine and **covert**
(And lucky no one fell
And broke an ankle in the dirt).

REMEMBER THIS:

Covert=under *cover*.

Now you:

_____

_____

_____

_____

_____

Cower

(verb) "KOW-er"

To **shrink away in shame or fear**
(I doubt any one of us hasn't been here).
When you **cower** you **tremble** and **wince**,
Maybe **crouch**,
So a **cowering posture**
Might cause you to **slouch**.

The Cowardly Lion, Dorothy's guy . . .
He **cowered** whenever monkeys flew by.
In his heart he was brave,
But he'd still **shake** and **twitch**
Whenever he dealt with
That nasty, green witch.

REMEMBER THIS:

A *coward* is likely to *cower*.

Now you:

_____

_____

_____

_____

_____

Cursory

(adj) "KER-ser-ee"

Cursory is **superficial**,
Incomplete and **quickly done**,
Like when you finish vacuuming
Right after you've begun.

In my first job I was a slob.
My **effort was the worst**.
My boss got tired and I was fired
But not before he cursed.

You'll get *curs*ed out for doing *curs*ory work.

Now you:

_____

_____

_____

_____

_____

Daft

(adj) "DAFT"

Crazy, stupid, foolish,
And **daffy**, like the duck
Who would irritate Bugs Bunny
Which was just the rabbit's luck.
As children we would watch him go,
And when he acted **daft**
(Getting into **stupid** trouble),
We all clapped our hands and laughed.

*Daff*y Duck was *daf*t.

Now you:

_____

_____

_____

_____

_____

Dearth

(noun) "DERTH"

It's a **scarcity**, a **shortage**,
A **running-low supply**.
We need much more efficient cars!
Have any guesses why?
We act like it's no problem,
But there seems to be a **dearth**
Of oil beneath the soil.
We have a **dearth** within the earth.

REMEMBER THIS:

There's a dearth of oil in the earth.

Now you:

_____

_____

_____

_____

_____

Decorous

(adj) "DEK-or-us"

Decorous people are **proper**.
They're **refined**
And **behave with decorum**.
But if someone is acting _too_ **decorous**
Just stick out your tongue
Or ignore 'em.

Picture an old navy captain
Whose crew is a pain in the neck;
If his sailors are being _in_**decorous**
He shoves them right off of the deck.

REMEMBER THIS:

Sailors should be _dec_orous on _deck_.

Now you:

_____

_____

_____

_____

_____

Defame

(verb) "Dih-FAME"

When you **defame**
You **trash someone's good name**.
You **slander**
And point the cold finger of **shame**.
See it this way:
It's like *taking the fame out*
(But at the same time
It's *not* taking the shame out).

REMEMBER THIS:

To defame is to trash someone's name,
to *de-famous* him.

Now you:

_____

_____

_____

_____

_____

Defunct

(adj) "Dih-FUNKT"

It's **expired**, **out of order**,
Not here anymore,
Not working, **not living**,
More dead than before.

Rick James was a singer who brought on
    the funk
In an era when people were dancing to
    punk.
He was funky . . .
With "Super Freak" he made a name,
But now he's de-funked, so that's it for
    Rick James.

REMEMBER THIS:

De funk singer is now *defunc*t.

Now you:

_____

_____

_____

_____

_____

D

Delectable

(adj) "Dih-LEKT-uh-bul"

It means **highly pleasing**, **enjoyable**.
It's something that's truly **delicious**.
If there's only one slice
Of **delectable** pizza,
Look out 'cause I get kind of vicious.

*Del*ectable is *del*icious.

Now you:

_____

_____

_____

_____

_____

Deleterious

(adj) "Del-ih-TEER-ee-us"

Now sit up straight
While I teach **deleterious**;
This is a word that is heavy and serious.
It's **hurtful** and **harmful**.
It's **just plain destructive**.
Deleterious types
    can be most unproductive.

Link it to terrorists;
It's nothing mysterious . . .
I'd like to delete them
'Cause they're **deleterious**.

Deleterious: think of *deleting terrorists*, who are destructive.

Now you:

_____

_____

_____

_____

_____

Depraved

(adj) "Dih-PRAYVED"

Perverted, wicked, and **corrupt** . . .
That defines **depraved**.
Depraved and **evil creeps** like Hitler
Simply can't be saved.

REMEMBER THIS:

Wickedness runs deep in a depraved person.
Get it? *Deep* in a *deep*raved person?

Now you:

_____

_____

_____

_____

_____

D

Derision

(noun) "Dih-RIH-zhun"

It's **making fun of someone.**
It's **mocking, ridicule.**
How much cold **derision**
Flies around inside your school?

Jon Stewart **mocks** celebrities.
He teases and **derides**.
He makes a ton of money
Being comical and **snide**.

But serious **derision**
Is like a mental incision.

REMEMBER THIS:

De*rision* is like a mental inc*ision*.

Now you:

_____

_____

_____

_____

_____

Derivative

(adj) "Dih-RIV-uh-tiv"

Derivative isn't original;
It's **derived from some earlier source**.
You've had exposure to this kind of thing
Just from listening to music, of course.

It seems that a lot of "new" songs
That I hear
Have been ripped
From some cool, older artist;
So many samples and riffs are just **copied**.
Creatively, that's not the smartest
(And really not trying your hardest).

*Deriv*ative work was *deriv*ed from something else.

Now you:

_____

_____

_____

_____

_____

Destitute

(adj) "DES-tih-toot"

Who watches *South Park*?
Do you know about Kenny?
That kid is **destitute**—
Can't spare a penny.
Poor and **impoverished**,
That's **destitute**.
Kenny lives in his parka,
Desperate for loot.

Destitute is desperate for loot.

Now you:

_____

_____

_____

_____

_____

Dilapidated

(adj) "Dih-LAP-ih-day-tid"

It's **trashed** and **broken down**,
So that **dilapidated** car—
The one that's **limping**, **slow**,
And groaning—
That won't get you very far.

Dilapi*dated*: think *dated* as in an old, junky car.

Now you:

_____

_____

_____

_____

_____

D

Dilatory

(adj) "DIL-uh-tory"

Dilatory people are **slow** and they're **late**.
That tired, old nonsense
Is something I hate.
"I couldn't find my keys!"
"I was straightening my hair!"
When it comes to excuses,
I really don't care.
I have an idea:
Let's charge a **late** fee:
You owe seven bucks
When you're **dilatory**!

*Dila*tory people *delay* everybody else.

Now you:

_____

_____

_____

_____

_____

Diminutive

(adj) "Dih-MIN-yuh-tiv"

Diminutive is **tiny**, and it could be cute.
It's really just another way to say **minute**
Which also means **small**.
I'm talking, **not tall**.
When **diminutives** trip,
They don't have far to fall.

Di*minut*ive=*minut*e.
(That's "my-NOOT," Chief.
If you pronounced it "minnit" you get a whack
on the head.)

Now you:

_____

_____

_____

_____

_____

Disconsolate

(adj) "Dis-KON-suh-lit"

Britney Spears fell **into a funk**
'Cause the press started calling her
"One crazy punk."
Does that make her **disconsolate**?
I doubt she's *that* **unhappy** yet.
Disconsolate's a little bold;
It means **you cannot be consoled**.

To help to keep her from **despair**,
I have advice I'd like to share:
Don't try to sing—do this instead:
Go raise your kids! Don't shave your head!

Dis*consol*ate=can't be *consol*ed.

Now you:

_____

_____

_____

_____

_____

Dissension

(noun) "Dih-SEN-shun"

So you caused a **debate**
In your history class—
You started a big **argument**.
That's called **dissension**
Which isn't all bad.
I guess it depends on intent.

Some people feel dissed by **dissension**,
But who says that friends should agree?
If there's no one to **challenge** you,
You'll be a bore,
Stuck and static indefinitely.

Some people feel *diss*ed by *diss*ension.

Now you:

_____

_____

_____

_____

_____

Divisive

(adj) "Dih-VICE-iv"

Some people are really **destructive** . . .
They try to **split** couples and teams.
They want to **tear you from your partner**
And **divide** you from your dreams.

I used to know a girl like this.
My friends called her "**The Splitter**."
She tried to take my boyfriend,
And I thought I'd have to hit her.

*Divi*sive people *divi*de situations.

Now you:

_____

_____

_____

_____

D

Dogmatic

(adj) "Dog-MAT-ik"

When you're **rigid with opinions**
And **you say what you think**,
You might be called **dogmatic**
Like a **preacher** or a shrink.

It can be annoying
When someone is too **dogmatic**.
It might be best if you suggest
She **preach** up in the attic.

*Dog*matic=attached to your ideas
like a *dog* with a bone.

Now you:

_____

_____

_____

_____

_____

Dolt

(noun) "DOELT"

A **dolt** is a **nitwit**, a **dull**, **stupid person**.
Hang out with **dolts**,
And your life will just worsen.
Poor old Marge Simpson
Woke up with a jolt
Realizing that she had just married a **dolt**.

Homer Simpson says "D'oh!" because he's
a dolt.

Now you:

_____

_____

_____

_____

_____

Dour

(adj) "DOW-er"

Sullen, **sour**, and **grumpy**
Is an attitude that's **dour**.
It's how I get from
Watching politicians for an hour.

Dour=sour.

Now you:

_____

_____

_____

_____

Duplicitous

(adj) "Doo-PLISS-it-iss"

Duplicitous people are **two-faced**.
You **can't be too sure where they stand**.
Duplicitous people will **lie** to you
While smiling and shaking your hand.

The word is like **dual** and **duplicate**.
See there, the reference to **two**?
These people are big **double dealers**.
They're **sneaky** and **lame** and **untrue**.

You read about Jack in *The Lord of the Flies*?
He's one of fiction's **duplicitous** guys.

*Du*plicitous people *du*pe you with their *dual* personalities.

Now you:

_____

_____

_____

_____

D

Eclectic

(adj) "Eh-KLEK-tik"

When you have **eclectic** taste,
You **choose from varied places**.
You shop around the world
To cover all the **different** bases.
If you have a bookshelf
That reflects a **wide selection**
That's **eclectic**,
And you should be proud of that collection.

Hendrix, Will I Am, Beethoven,
Coldplay and The Fixx . . .
I'd define that playlist
As a cool, **eclectic mix**.

REMEMBER THIS:

Eclectic—think "collect."
If you have e*clect*ic taste you have a varied *collect*ion.

Now you:

_____

_____

_____

_____

_____

Efface

(verb) "Eh-FASE"

It's another of the easy rhymes
Within this vocab mission
'Cause **efface** rhymes with **erase**,
And **erase** is the definition.

REMEMBER THIS:

Efface means erase.

Now you:

_____

_____

_____

_____

_____

Efficacious

(adj) "Ef-ih-KAY-shus"

Efficacious:
Producing desired effect . . .
Okay, that word seems to make sense.
You see the **effect** in there
And you see **effort**.
Get it?
I knew you weren't dense.

Hey, what about that Oprah Winfrey?
She's **hard working** and she is gracious.
She tends to **deliver desired results**,
So we can call her **efficacious**.

*Effic*acious things produce desired *effec*ts.

Now you:

_____

_____

_____

_____

_____

Effrontery

(noun) "Eh-FRUNT-er-ee"

Shamelessness, boldness,
And **blatant audacity** . . .
These words add up to **effrontery**.
So last night I went out
To watch a new film,
And a huge girl sat down
Right in front of me.
She was tall with a hat.
I said, "What's up with that?"
Why are some people so **rude**?
So I drummed on her chair
'Til she got outta there.
That did a lot for my mood.

She had the *effront*ery to sit right *in front* of me.

Now you:

_____

_____

_____

_____

_____

E

Egregious

(adj) "Eh-GREE-jus"

Egregious refers to something
That's **really**, **really bad**,
Like the **worst** kind of mistake,
Or the **worst** date you ever had.

A surgeon's **egregious** error
Could cause someone to die.
If you say, "I authored *Hamlet*,"
That's an **egregious** lie.

E*gre*gious errors can cause *grie*f.

Now you:

_____

_____

_____

_____

_____

Emaciated

(adj) "Ee-MAY-shee-ay-tid"

Abnormally thin, just **wasting away**.
It really adds up to no good.
When I hear the word **emaciated**
These days
Someone's talking about Hollywood.
Why are these actresses so freaking **thin**?
They look like they're **hungry** and **sick**.
Why would you want to be Lollipop Head
Or to look like a wig on a stick?

Emaciated is underweighted.

Now you:

_____

_____

_____

_____

_____

Emblematic

(adj) "Em-bleh-MAT-ik"

It's something that's **symbolic**
And can **stand for something else**.
A peace sign **symbolizes** peace,
Mercedes logo: wealth.
Those two signs look much the same,
And they're both **emblematic**,
Yet one says money, one says peace . . .
Does that seem problematic?

REMEMBER THIS:

*Emblem*atic has to do with *emblem*s.

Now you:

_____

_____

_____

_____

_____

Eminent

(adj) "EM-ih-nent"

If you're **highly praised within your field**,
Think of the power you could wield.
Eminence is **celebrated**,
Prominent, and **highly rated**.

You know the rapper Eminem . . .
His tattooed fans think he's a gem.
Slim Shady gets to rant and vent;
Success has made him **eminent**.

REMEMBER THIS:

*Emin*em is *emin*ent in rap.

Now you:

_____

_____

_____

_____

_____

E

Enervate

(verb) "EN-er-vate"

This word used to confuse me.
It's meaning is not what I guessed.
It *doesn't* mean to **energize**;
It's more like to **drain** or **depress**.

To **enervate** just means to **weaken**,
To **suck all the energy from**.
Like Kryptonite **weakening** Superman.
Lucky him, he recharges with sun.

REMEMBER THIS:

Enervate: the *opposite* of energize.

Now you:

_____

_____

_____

_____

_____

Enmity

(noun) "EN-mih-tee"

Do you know anyone who's a total creep?
Do you **despise** him so much
That you're losing sleep?
If you feel this kind of **hostility**,
That's complete and total **enmity**.

I feel **enmity**
For people who lie and sneak
And some politicians and terrorist freaks.
My **enmity** list is kind of slim.
Oh yeah, O. J. Simpson—
Can't forget him.

REMEMBER THIS:

You feel *en*mity for your *en*emies.

Now you:

_____

_____

_____

_____

_____

Ennui

(noun) "On-WEE"

Well, how cool are you
To know a word like this?
We stole it from the French
(Like we stole the French Kiss).
It's a **feeling of boredom**—
It's a **lack of any ZING**!
When you're hit with **ennui**,
You don't want to do a thing.

I feel *ennui* (On-WEE) *on wee*kends.

Now you:

_____

_____

_____

_____

_____

Ensconced

(adj) "En-SKONST"

When you're **tightly tucked in**,
Then you are **ensconced**.
It basically means that you're **snug**.
You know that old saying that
    grandparents use:
"He's **ensconced** as a bug in a rug"?

The Midwest is **cozy,** so try to remember
The words of the great Andrew Johnson:
"I can't think of anywhere I'd rather be
Than **ensconced** by a lake in Wisconsin."
*Then again, Andrew Johnson probably
    never said anything like that.*

It's cozy to be en*scon*ced in Wi*scon*sin.

Now you:

_____

_____

_____

_____

_____

E

Envenom

(verb) "En-VEN-um"

It means to **poison**, to **cause bitterness**,
To **create a really bad feeling**.
The damage can end up so awfully bad
That there's almost no hope for the healing.

First, you may use the word literally:
"Snakes have **envenomed** that dude,"
Or use it as if it's a metaphor,
Then sit back and see if you're sued:
"Calvin Klein, he had a plot . . .
He plotted to **envenom** . . .
He sneaked into Armani's shop
And stole Giorgio's denim."

REMEMBER THIS:

En*venom*=to poison, as with *venom*.

Now you:

_____

_____

_____

_____

_____

Ephemeral

(adj) "Eh-FEM-er-ul"

Okay, I'm not a big fan of TV,
And I *am* pretty lazy with food,
But there's something about
That guy Emeril
That just puts me in a good mood.
So I hope that he won't be **ephemeral**
Which is **lasting a very short time**
Because someday I'd like to see
More in my fridge
Than a case of Corona and lime.

REMEMBER THIS:

I hope E*meril* won't be eph*emeral*.

Now you:

_____

_____

_____

_____

_____

Erroneous

(adj) "Eh-RONE-ee-us"

It's **inaccurate, false, wrong, untrue**.
I'd say that covers it, wouldn't you?
I cannot say it any sparer:
Erroneous defines an error.

*Err*oneous=an *err*or.

Now you:

_____

_____

_____

_____

_____

Erudite

(adj) "AIR-yoo-dite"

Erudite—this word is tight.
It's **smart** and **educated**.
Erudite book lovers
Are the only guys I dated.

This is a vocab word
With which you should acquaint
'Cause if you can't define it,
Then **erudite** you ain't.

Erudite means very bright.

Now you:

_____

_____

_____

_____

_____

E

Espouse
(verb) "Eh-SPOWZ"

To **support**, **stand behind**,
And to **take up a cause**.
Karl **espoused** communism
Despite all its flaws.

Espousing means
Giving your loyalty to,
So **espousing** your spouse
Is a good thing to do.

It's a good idea to e*spouse* your *spouse*.

Now you:

_____

_____

_____

_____

_____

Ethereal
(adj) "Ih-THEER-ee-ul"

Delicate, **vapory**, **not of this world** . . .
Ethereal feelings are **airy**.
I once felt **ethereal**, sick with the flu,
I was dizzy and **light**, **like a fairy**.

This word comes right out of the ether,
Which the doc sniffed in *Cider House Rules*.
It made him lightheaded,
Then dead, as we dreaded.
Sometimes even doctors are fools.

Think "ether-real." . . .
Ethereal feels unreal, as if under the effects of
ether.

Now you:

_____

_____

_____

_____

_____

Euphemism

(noun) "YOO-fuh-miz-um"

It's a **mild or sweet expression**
To replace one that's too strong.
We've all been taught to use them,
And we all just play along.
People say *full figured*
When they're really saying *fat*.
Restroom means *the toilet*,
And I'm quite okay with that.

There are many **euphemisms**
Used to mean you're dead,
Like *kicked the bucket*, *passed away*,
And *being put to bed*.
These are used in eulogies
When speaking to the crowd
'Cause "That guy's dead" is just too harsh,
So that one's not allowed.

REMEMBER THIS:

*Eu*phemisms are *u*sed in *eu*logies.

Now you:

_____

_____

_____

_____

_____

Exacerbate

(verb) "Ex-ASS-er-bate"

When you **exacerbate** a problem,
You only **make it worse**,
Like driving to a funeral,
Then smashing up the hearse.

If you get caught within a lie
And still continue to deny,
You **exacerbate** the mess.
Save your butt and just confess.

REMEMBER THIS:

His constant *exac*erbation caused his Mom's *exas*peration.

Now you:

_____

_____

_____

_____

_____

E

Exemplary

(adj) "Ex-EMP-luh-ree"

Exemplary behavior deserves **imitation**.
Exemplary people receive admiration
Or set **bad** examples:
In Young Hollywood
They **teach** how to *screw up* careers,
And for good.
Miss Lohan's bad headlines
Are too often true;
Such **exemplary** girls
Teach us what *not* to do.

*Exemp*lary=sets an *examp*le.

Now you:

_____

_____

_____

_____

_____

Expedient

(adj) "Ex-PEED-ee-ent"

It's when something is **to your advantage**
Or **gets what you need** when you need it.
When your stomach tells you it's hungry,
It's **expedient** for you to feed it.

There's this website,
And it's called Expedia;
You buy tickets for hotels and planes.
Get it? It's helping you **get what you want**
When you want to see Scotland or Spain.
(*Or Egypt. Or Cleveland. Or Tasmania.*
Or anyplace else I didn't mention because
*   they don't rhyme with* plane!)

*Exped*ia is an *exped*ient travel website.

Now you:

_____

_____

_____

_____

Expound

(verb) "Ex-POWND"

This means to **explain**.
It means to **get the point across**,
To **clarify**, to **say a little more**.
If you have complaints
And you **expound** them for the boss,
Make it quick. Don't be a thumping bore.
So here's a quick mnemonic . . .
Kind of simple, kind of plain . . .
Expounding is like *pounding*
Your ideas in my brain.

Ex*pounding* is like *pounding* an idea.

Now you:

_____

_____

_____

_____

_____

Expunge

(verb) "Ex-PUNJ"

Expunging means **erasing**,
Wiping out, destroying.
Why not just **expunge**
The things you do that are annoying?

There are people in this world
I wish we could **expunge**.
Paris Hilton, for example—
It's time she took a plunge.

E*xpunge* is to wipe out, as you do with a *sponge*.

Now you:

_____

_____

_____

_____

_____

E

Expurgate

(verb) "EX-per-gate"

Aggressive expurgation
Is one way to **amend**.
You **cut out words and phrases**
That might shock or might offend.

The show you love on cable
Makes your father yell, "X rated!"
I'll bet you don't agree about
What should be **expurgated**.

REMEMBER THIS:

Ex*purg*ate means to *purge*.
(See "purge" in the word?)

Now you:

_____

_____

_____

_____

_____

Façade

(noun) "Fuh-SOD"

The **decorative front of a building**
Is something we call a **façade**,
But **façade** also means **fake
    appearance**,
And that's when it gets kind of odd . . .
It can *literally* be on a building:
The **façade** was destroyed in the quake.
But when *someone* puts on a **façade**,
Then look out 'cause that person is **fake**.

REMEMBER THIS:

Façade=false face.

Now you:

_____

_____

_____

_____

_____

Facetious

(adj) "Fuh-SEE-shus"

Facetious comments are **meant to amuse**,
But sometimes
They might end up causing a bruise,
Like calling from deep in the crowd,
"Hey Obama,"
And screaming out insults that start with
"Yo Mama."

Know this: when someone's **facetious**,
He's **joking**.
The comments are **humor**
But could be provoking.
You might keep your attitude light,
Just in case
'Cause you can't see **facetiousness**
On someone's face.

REMEMBER THIS:

You might not see *face*tiousness on my *face*.

Now you:

_____

_____

_____

_____

_____

Facile

(adj) "FAS-il"

So **facile** means **easy**.
How hard is that?
A **facile** achievement
Takes no time flat.

Facil in Spanish
Means **easy** too,
So now you're bilingual.
Whoopdee bueno for you.

REMEMBER THIS:

Facile . . . think *faci*litator,
    whose job it is to make things easier.

Now you:

_____

_____

_____

_____

_____

F

Fallacious

(adj) "Fuh-LAY-shus"

The tabloids are **fallacious**.
They're **misleading**, **full of lies**.
They're papers full of **falsehoods**.
This writing I despise.
I have an idea . . .
Why don't we try it?
When a magazine's **fallacious**,
Just don't buy it!

Fallacious means false.

Now you:

_____

_____

_____

_____

_____

Fatuous

(adj) "FAT-yoo-us"

Fatuous fatheads are **foolish** and **silly**.
Have you heard of the "singers"
Called Milli Vanilli?
They were two long-haired
And **fatuous** guys
Stripped of their Grammys
Because of their lies.
That's pretty **fatuous**—
What were they thinking?
Pretending to sing
But instead just lip synching . . .

Fatuous=Fathead.

Now you:

_____

_____

_____

_____

_____

Feckless

(adj) "FEK-less"

It means **irresponsible**, **careless** . . .
In need of a lot more direction.
If your nurses are messy and **feckless**
You might get a raging infection.

Fecklessness mirrors **indifference**,
So I guess if you're **lazy** and **feckless**,
You're really a **slacker** and kind of a hacker
And likely to be pretty **reckless**.

REMEMBER THIS:

Being feckless can be pretty reckless.

Now you:

_____

_____

_____

_____

_____

Feign

(verb) "FANE"

It's to **make believe**, **pretend**.
It's essentially to **fake**.
Ferris Bueller **feigned** a whole day ill,
That crafty little snake.

When Madonna moved to England,
We crowned her Queen of **Feigning**.
An English accent _in one week_?
Very entertaining.

REMEMBER THIS:

To feign is to fake.

Now you:

_____

_____

_____

_____

_____

F

Felicity

(noun) "Fel-ISS-ih-tee"

"**Feliz** Navidad" plays each Christmas,
But only last year I discerned
These **happy** old lyrics were teaching me
The first Spanish I ever learned.
Feliz is just Spanish for **happy**.
And **felicity**—that's **happiness**,
It's **joyfulness** and it's **contentment**,
Like a love life without any stress.

REMEMBER THIS:

"Feliz Navidad" is wishing you felicity.

Now you:

_____

_____

_____

_____

_____

Feral

(adj) "FARE-ul"

It's **undomesticated**.
It's **wild** and **untamed**.
A pack of **feral** dogs
Might leave you chewed up and maimed.

A student once explained it:
"Listen, this is the deal:
It's almost as if **feral**
Just means something's **for real**.
Like—**in a natural state**
Before you're taught how to act.
When you're **feral** you're **for real**
With all your **wildness** intact."

REMEMBER THIS:

Feral=for real.

Now you:

_____

_____

_____

_____

_____

Fervor

(noun) "FER-ver"

It's a **great passion**,
A **strong**, **intense heat**.
His **fervor** for watching the Mets
Is complete.
He's their biggest fan.
He's a **fervid** believer.
Yankee fans think
He has some kind of **fever**.

His fervor gave him a fever.

Now you:

_____

_____

_____

_____

_____

Fictitious

(adj) "Fik-TISH-us"

False and **fake**, yep, that's **fictitious**.
Uh oh,
Here comes something vicious:
Pamela Anderson . . . oh my god!
That is one **fictitious** broad.
Is any part of her for real?
Maybe a kneecap or a heel.
What does she look like in the morning?
Don't sneak up without fair warning.

_Fict_itious is _fict_ional.

Now you:

_____

_____

_____

_____

_____

F

Flagrant

(adj) "FLAY-grent"

Shockingly glaring or **obvious**.
My basketball coach had to howl
When another guard elbowed me
Right in the jaw.
That was a big **flagrant** foul.

Some people are quite patriotic,
So much that they lecture and nag.
To them,
The most **flagrant** offense you can do
Is to burn an American flag.

Some think it's a *flagr*ant offense to burn a *flag*.

Now you:

_____

_____

_____

_____

_____

Flippant

(adj) "FLIP-ent"

It's **disrespectful**. Oh, it's **rude**
And shows **you won't be serious**.
It's a **rebel's attitude** . . .
(My **flippancy** makes me delirious).

If someone dares to flip you off,
That's **flippant**, and to boot
They're really kinda swearing.
It's the one-finger salute.

*Flip*ping someone off is *flip*pant.

Now you:

_____

_____

_____

_____

_____

Fortuitous

(adj) "For-TOO-it-us"

**A stroke of lucky fortune,
By accident, by chance.**
If you're pleasant *and* **fortuitous**,
You might just find romance.

With only seven seconds left,
I stole and dunked the ball,
But that was thanks to practice—
Not **fortuitous** at all.

REMEMBER THIS:

Something *fortu*itous is a stroke of good *fortu*ne.

Now you:

_____

_____

_____

_____

_____

Frenetic

(adj) "Freh-NET-ik"

When you're **wildly excited**
And **acting all nutty,**
You're **frenetic** and **frantic**.
Knock it off, Buddy.
I'm trying to study.

REMEMBER THIS:

Frantic + Energetic = Frenetic.

Now you:

_____

_____

_____

_____

_____

F

Frugal

(adj) "FROO-gul"

When you're **frugal** with your money,
You are **careful not to waste** it.
You're **saving** for a car—
A goal so close you almost taste it.
It's not the same as being cheap;
Cheap people just won't spend.
Frugality won't let you *waste*
(And may not let you lend).

REMEMBER THIS:

It can be frugal to shop through Google.

Now you:

_____

_____

_____

_____

_____

Furtive

(adj) "FER-tiv"

Sneaky and **sly** is a **furtive** guy.
When your wallet goes missing,
You'll know why.

The wolf was very **furtive**
As he tricked Miss Riding Hood.
He snacked on poor old Grandma,
But the hunter got him good.

REMEMBER THIS:

*Fur*tive, like a sneaky, *fur*ry wolf.

Now you:

_____

_____

_____

_____

_____

Garner

(verb) "GAR-ner"

When you **garner** you **gather**,
You **collect** and you **store**.
What secret things are **garnered**
In your underwear drawer?
What if I came over there
And opened it now?
Or better yet, your mother . . .
Would she scream and have a cow?

A *gard*ener *gar*ners things in the *gar*den.

Now you:

_____

_____

_____

_____

_____

Garrulous

(adj) "GARE-uh-lus"

Have you heard of Gary Coleman
From the old show *Diff'rent Strokes*?
He was **garrulous**
With lots of **wordy**, **talky** jokes.
Garrulous is **chatty**.
Gary had to **yak** and boast.
"Whatchoo talking 'bout Willis?"
Is the line he **chattered** most.

*Gar*y Coleman was *garr*ulous on *Diff'rent Strokes*.

Now you:

_____

_____

_____

_____

_____

G

Girth

(noun) "GERTH"

Girth is **the distance around a thing**,
A simple kind of **measuring**.
Post-holiday **circumference**
Around your waist can be immense.
Is all that ham and cheesecake worth
The massive January **girth**?

REMEMBER THIS:

If you're going to give birth, expect some girth.

Now you:

_____

_____

_____

_____

_____

Glean

(verb) "GLEEN"

To **collect information**,
To **gather it slowly**
That is an act we call **gleaning**.
You're simply **discovering**,
Figuring out,
Trying to draw out the meaning.

When I was a kidlet, I wanted to **glean**
Who got that Tower of Pisa to lean?

REMEMBER THIS:

Try to glean what I mean.

Now you:

_____

_____

_____

_____

_____

Glutton

(noun) "GLUT-in"

Gluttony, gluttony . . .
Boy, oh boy
It's one of the deadly sins.
Stuff your big face like a **glutton**,
My friend,
And you'll soon have a nice triple chin.
Someone who eat and drinks
Way, way too much—
That's a guy we call a **glutton**.
Keep it up, Dude . . .
I don't mean to be rude,
But you're bound to pop all of your buttons.

REMEMBER THIS:

A glutton is going to pop a button.

Now you:

_____
_____
_____
_____
_____

Goad

(verb) "GODE"

To **prompt** and **persuade**
And **move someone along**.
I **goaded** Bob Dylan to write me a song.
Okay, that's not true.
Making lies up is wrong . . .
Who **goaded** you into
That gold-plated thong?

Enough about you.
Let's discuss the princess. Her heart
Was in shambles, her love life a mess.
But no matter how she might grovel or **goad**
She just couldn't fashion
A prince from a toad.

REMEMBER THIS:

To _go_ad is to get someone to _go_.

Now you:

_____
_____
_____
_____
_____

G

Gratifying
(adj) "GRAT-ih-fy-ing"

Something that **makes you**
Feel grateful . . .
And something that is **satisfying** . . .
And something that simply is **pleasing** . . .
That thing is called **gratifying**.

When I was a volleyball player,
Nothing was more **gratifying**
Than spiking
And knocking a girl off her feet.
If I said it felt bad, I'd be lying.

REMEMBER THIS:

You feel *grat*eful for things that are *grat*ifying.

Now you:

_____

_____

_____

_____

_____

Gregarious
(adj) "Greh-GARE-ee-us"

If a person's very **friendly**
And **outgoing**, he's **gregarious**.
A preacher who's **gregarious**
Might be the one to marry us
And someday even bury us.

Have you ever watched *The Brady Bunch*?
Come on! That show's a classic.
But if you're really young,
The Seventies might seem jurassic.

So what about Greg Brady?
He was always so **gregarious**:
Genial and **social**,
Though his clothes were just hilarious.

REMEMBER THIS:

Greg Brady was *greg*arious.

Now you:

_____

_____

_____

_____

_____

Hackneyed

(adj) "HACK-need"

Hackneyed expressions are
Boring and **common**,
Banal, clichéd, and **cheap**.
When writing is **hackneyed**,
We've heard it before.
Blah-blah-blah
Put me to sleep.

I'll tell you what's **hackneyed**:
Reality shows . . .
They're **worn out** and **lame** and all fake.
It's as I predicted:
The stuff that's depicted
Is **stale** and can't keep me awake.

If you write a *hack*neyed TV show, you're
a *hack*.

Now you:

_____

_____

_____

_____

_____

Hapless

(adj) "HAP-less"

Charlie Brown was what you'd call
A pretty **hapless** kid—
Unlucky and **unfortunate**,
No matter what he did.
Remember when he trusted Lucy
With that old football?
Mid-kick she'd snatch the ball away,
And **haplessly** he'd fall.

Hapless is unlucky, kind of like helpless.

Now you:

_____

_____

_____

_____

_____

Harangue

(noun) "Huh-RANG"

It's a **passionate speech**.
Maybe **angry**, with slang.
You know it when you hear it . . .
Not "Hooray!" It's **harangue**!

The Grinch's dog Max
Had the worst of careers;
Those Grinchy **harangues**
Always rang in his ears.

The Grinch's ha*rang*ues *rang* in Max's ears.

Now you:

_____

_____

_____

_____

_____

Heath, Heathen

(nouns) "HEETH" "HEE-then"

Here comes a twist. Maybe this will be fun:
I'm going to teach you two words in one.
Add **heathen** and **heath**
To your new knowledge base.
One is a person and one is a place.

A **heath** is a section of **overgrown land**
While a **heathen** is an **uncivilized man**.
Heath—that can also mean
"**Wild growing plant**."
Heathens don't worship.
Don't ask one to chant.

My sister's a rebel and sure as I'm breathin',
She'd love to hang out on a **heath**
With a **heathen**.

A heath: think wild-growing wreath.

A heathen probably isn't going to heaven.

Now you:

_____

_____

_____

_____

Heinous

(adj) "HAY-nus"

Heinous deeds are **shocking**.
They're **evil**, **awful**, **bad**.
And if I write the clue I want,
I'll make your mother mad.
So I'll just leave it here for now:
Oh, wouldn't it be **heinous**
To find your spaceship left you
All alone upon Uranus?

It would be heinous to be stuck on Uranus.

Now you:

_____

_____

_____

_____

_____

Hellion

(noun) "HELL-yun"

A **hellion** is a **rowdy one**.
He's **troublesome**, **bad**.
"Don't date any **hellions**,"
Begged my poor, nervous dad.

I guess it's **bad** if you are labeled
One of the **hellions**,
But history shows
Those people throw
The best of rebellions.

You can count on a hellion to start a rebellion.

Now you:

_____

_____

_____

_____

_____

Hiatus

(noun) "Hy-ATE-us"

It's a **rest**, it's a **vacation**,
It's some **time away from work**.
Bosses hate us on **hiatus**,
So just hit the road and smirk.

Bosses hate us for going on hiatus.

Now you:

_____

_____

_____

_____

_____

Humdrum

(adj) "HUM-drum"

Humdrum simply means
Dull or **boring**.
When your classes are **humdrum**,
You might end up snoring.

Ho hum, this class is humdrum.

Now you:

_____

_____

_____

_____

_____

Iconoclast

(noun) "Eye-KON-oe-klast"

Iconoclastic people
Don't follow the crowd.
They think that's mindless,
So that's not allowed.

They challenge the White House
And **question** your church;
They think we need answers;
Iconoclasts search.

Parents of this kind of child used to cope
By stuffing his mouth
With a big bar of soap.

Think **iconoCLASH**;
An iconoclast clashes with icons.

Now you:

_____

_____

_____

_____

_____

Illusory

(adj) "Ih-LOO-zuh-ree"

You know that David Blaine guy?
The magician on TV?
He **deceives**
And makes things seem **unreal**,
So he's **illusory**.

Makeup is **illusory**.
Some girls paint it thick,
And when they take it off,
Whoa,
"Who are *you*? Is this a trick??"

Illusory refers to an illusion.

Now you:

_____

_____

_____

_____

_____

Illustrious

(adj) "Il-US-tree-us"

Famous, distinguished,
And **highly regarded**.
Illustrious people are **known**.
Elizabeth the First was **illustrious** . . .
Thanks to forty-five years on the throne.

Have you read *The Polar Express*?
Chris Van Allsburg is its creator.
I love that magical fantasy tale,
And his paintings make it even greater.
(So aside from writing a really good book,
He's an **illustrious** book illustrator.)

REMEMBER THIS:

Van Allsburg is an *illustr*ious *illustr*ator.

Now you:

_____

_____

_____

_____

_____

Immaterial

(adj) "Im-uh-TEER-ee-ul"

It means **unimportant**,
Of no consequence.
There's so much in the news
It's intense.
The tabloids are rags that have
Nothing to say, so they publish
The **dumbest reports** of the day:

"Princess Diana Played Drums in Havana!"
"Hannah Montana Seen Eating Banana!"

My grandmother said, if I clearly recall,
"If there's **nothing to say**,
Then say nothing at all."

REMEMBER THIS:

So desperate for *material* they print the *immaterial*.

Now you:

_____

_____

_____

_____

_____

Imminent

(adj) "IM-ih-nint"

It's **just about to happen**,
It's **impending**, it's **near**.
If you're in **imminent** danger,
Grab your purse, get outta here.

It's down to one putt;
It's **imminent** that I'll win.
I'm **making it happen**.
In other words, *I'm in*.

If it's *immin*ent, *I'm in it.*

Now you:

_____

_____

_____

_____

_____

Impasse

(noun) "IM-pass"

It's a **place you can't get past**.
It's a **stalemate**,
A **dead end**.
Have you ever hit an **impasse**
With a parent or a friend?

Learn to pass an **impasse**;
Don't let yourself be **stuck**.
If you never learn to compromise,
Your life is gonna suck.

If you're stuck and can't *pass*, you're at an
impasse.

Now you:

_____

_____

_____

_____

_____

Impeccable

(adj) "Im-PEK-uh-bul"

Impeccable means that you have
Not a flaw.
It speaks of **perfection**
And leaves me in awe.
Impeccable manners,
Impeccable clothes.
You admire my **impeccable** taste,
I suppose.

Remember this word by remembering *peck.*
Whenever you peck,
You're a pain in the neck.
If someone's **impeccable**,
Don't bother pecking.
It's really your own peace of mind
That you're wrecking.

REMEMBER THIS:

We *peck* even im*pecc*able people.

Now you:

_____

_____

_____

_____

_____

Imperious

(adj) "Im-PEER-ee-us"

Imperious people are **arrogant, lordly.**
They **think they deserve the best things.**
Put simply, they act all **imperial**
Like big **snotty** princes and kings.

Just spit on the people
Who think they're **imperious**.
I know that it's crude,
But I'm totally serious.

REMEMBER THIS:

*Imperi*ous people act *imperi*al.

Now you:

_____

_____

_____

_____

_____

Impregnable

(adj) "Im-PREG-nuh-bul"

Oh, I'm gonna get it for this one,
But how can I not spell it out?
Impregnable means
That you're **safe from attack**,
And you're thinking of "pregnant,"
No doubt.

So a bird cannot catch
An **impregnable** worm;
An **impregnable** egg will be **safe**
From a sperm.

Impregnable=can't be attacked, can't get
    pregnant . . . whatever.

Now you:

_____

_____

_____

_____

_____

Improvident

(adj) "Im-PROV-ih-dent"

When you're **failing to save**
For your needs down the road,
You're **improvident** and you're **unwary**.
My cousin will buy only Prada.
She's **improvident**,
So much it's scary.

Big spending might lead her to poverty;
She just spent two grand on a purse.
I *used* to think she was **improvident**,
But now that girl's twenty times worse.

If you're im*prov*ident you might end up in
    *pov*erty.

Now you:

_____

_____

_____

_____

_____

Impudent

(adj) "IMP-yoo-dent"

Have you ever heard someone
Call someone an imp?
It's a **pixie**, a **rascal**, a **brat**.
And that's how you act if you're **impudent**.
How totally simple is that?
You're **cocky**, **smart-alecky**, **flippant**,
So you might be an **impudent** imp
If you run around setting off fire alarms
Or call your math teacher a wimp.

REMEMBER THIS:

An *imp*udent kid acts like an *imp*.

Now you:

_____

_____

_____

_____

_____

Inane

(adj) "In-ANE"

Inane is just **foolish**. **In**ane is **so dumb**.
Inane is what people with fame
Can become.
Have you heard what these actors
Are naming their kids?
These **inane** people are losing their lids:
Apple and Lyric and Banjo and Slate . . .
A girl named Blowdryer is next,
Just you wait.
Hey, why not just name your kid
Childbirthing Pain?
Why are these people so freaking **inane**?

REMEMBER THIS:

Celebrity kid *name*s are i*nane* and in*sane*.

Now you:

_____

_____

_____

_____

_____

Incongruous

(adj) "In-KON-groo-us"

I looked in a thesaurus
And here is what it said:
Inconsistent, laughable—
Just like a stupid head.
It's **screwy** and **illogical**,
Twisted and **absurd**.
Look at all those synonyms
For just one little word.

How perfect, it occurred to me:
That's just like government.
The congress is **incongruous**.
When will they represent?

REMEMBER THIS:

In *Congress* they can be pretty in*congruous*.

Now you:

_____
_____
_____
_____
_____

Indefatigable

(adj) "In-dee-FAT-ih-guh-bul"

Say that *one out loud a few times*!
An **indefatigable** person
Never seems to get tired.
This is the kind of **high-energy** freak
Whom I have long admired.
'Cause I'm into big-time napping, myself.
Don't mess with my sleep.
If I don't crash at least nine hours,
I'm **zippy** as a sheep.

REMEMBER THIS:

Inde*fatig*able: see "*fatigue*" in the word?
  You know, tired . . .

Now you:

_____
_____
_____
_____
_____

Indolent

(adj) "IN-doe-lent"

Indolent people are totally **lazy**.
If you want to work hard,
They think you're half crazy.

You know how kids abbreviate?
With "aggro" and "emo?"
Let's make up one for **lazy**
Using **indolent**—"Indo"!
"When I feel really indo,
I just stare out the window."
(*Yeah, it's stupid,*
   but I'll bet you're stuck with it now.)

When I feel indo, I stare out the window.

Now you:

_____

_____

_____

_____

_____

Inert

(adj) "In-ERT"

Inactive, **sluggish**, as **peppy as a log**.
When you're feeling **inert**,
You're a **lazy,** old dog.
You learned **inertia** in science:
You know: "A body **at rest** . . ."
It's about **resisting motion**
(No, there won't be a test).

Inert=inertia.

Now you:

_____

_____

_____

_____

_____

Inestimable

(adj) "In-ES-tih-muh-bul"

It's **too much to estimate**,
Too high to guess.
My **inestimable** wealth is like Sting's,
More or less.

I **wonder how much** cash
George Lucas has earned,
How much *Indiana* and *Star Wars* returned.
He wrote and produced,
So his pockets are full.
His wealth at this point is **inestimable**.

In*estim*able is too high to *estima*te.

Now you:

_____

_____

_____

_____

_____

Inevitable

(adj) "In-EV-ih-tuh-bul"

It's **destined to happen**. It's **on**. It's **a go**.
Don't wonder about it; you already know.
It's **something impending**.
It's as you **incited** it.
Inevitably,
It's **as if you invited it**.

Big Humpty Dumpty, he sat on a wall?
No wonder the idiot had a great fall.
He was probably drinking or tired or full.
That drop on the head was **inevitable**.

If it's inevitable, it's like you invited it to happen, like you sent it an Evite . . . see "evite" in the word??

Now you:

_____

_____

_____

_____

_____

Inflammable

(adj) "In-FLAM-uh-bul"

This word is just nutty
(English language is cracked).
It means the *same* as **flammable**.
Is that not totally whacked?

Inflammable materials
Can burst into flame.
And ***flammable***,
Well, that word means exactly the same.
So even with the prefix "in,"
It still ***can be* ignited**.
The makers of this language
Should be rounded up and bited.

In*flamm*able and *flamm*able *BOTH* mean
flame-able.
Whatever.

Now you:

_____

_____

_____

_____

_____

Inoperable

(adj) "In-OP-er-uh-bul"

It means they just **can't operate**.
The **surgeon can't get at it**.
That knee wound is **inoperable**?
Your ballet days have had it.

You can't *opera*te on something in*opera*ble.

Now you:

_____

_____

_____

_____

_____

Inquisitive

(adj) "In-KWIZ-ih-tiv"

If you like to **inquire**
Or **ask lots of questions**,
You like a good **inquisition**.
Remember the King's **Inquisition** in
    Spain?
Have you read about *that* nutty mission?

Inquisitive people are **curious**,
But **curiosity**, that "killed the cat."
(Who'd make up a phrase so injurious?
What kind of weirdo does that?)

*Inqui*sitive people are always *quiz*zing and
    *inqui*ring.

Now you:

_____

_____

_____

_____

_____

Insipid

(adj) "In-SIP-id"

Insipid—that's **uninteresting**.
It's **tasteless** and it's **bland**.
Why you date **insipid** girls
I'll never understand.

Insipid—that's like wheat grass.
'Cause yuck, it **has no flavor**.
Dump it in your friend's back seat,
And do yourself a favor.

Don't *sip* an in*sip*id drink.

Now you:

_____

_____

_____

_____

_____

Insolent

(adj) "IN-soe-lent"

Chris Rock as we know
Can be pretty **rude**
And **insulting**.
That makes him an **insolent** dude.
He's off-the-charts funny
And just a bit **crude**.
Less **insolence** would help the world.
I don't doubt it.
But stand-up comedy
Would sure suck without it.

REMEMBER THIS:

*Ins*olent is *ins*ulting.

Now you:

_____

_____

_____

_____

_____

Insular

(adj) "IN-suh-ler"

Detached and **narrow minded**,
And even **isolated**.
Insular and **cliquey** girls
Are highly overrated.

If you hang
With just your people every single day,
You're kind of **insulated**.
What more is there to say?

REMEMBER THIS:

If you're *insul*ar, you're *insulat*ing yourself.

Now you:

_____

_____

_____

_____

_____

Insurgence

(noun) "In-SER-jents"

It's an **act of rebellion**, **revolt**,
Demonstration.
Okay, here's my moment
To vent some frustration:
When will you guys start **rebelling**,
Protesting?
Your whole generation
Just seems to be resting.
You've heard of the Sixties?
Those people spoke out.
They taught us
What freedom of speech is about.
Come on. Let's get up.
Though it might sound deranged,
Sometimes **insurgence**
Is needed for **change**.

REMEMBER THIS:

An in*surge*nce involves a forward *surge*.

Now you:

_____

_____

_____

_____

_____

I

Intrepid

(adj) "In-TREP-id"

Intrepid means **courageous** and **bold**.
If you're young, scared, weak, or old—
Stand up—don't always do as you're told.

Remember Atticus,
In *To Kill a Mockingbird*?
He showed you what it means to be
Intrepid with your word.

REMEMBER THIS:

Intrepid—It's *not* tepid. *(Great, s*o what's tepid??
It's halfhearted, mushy, lukewarm. *Not* intrepid.)

Now you:

_____

_____

_____

_____

_____

Inundate

(verb) "IN-un-date"

If you're **flooded** and you're
Overwhelmed,
Then you are **inundated**.
Don't **inundate** with cheap cologne.
That *can't* be overstated.

Inundated with nice jewelry,
Inundated with hot dates,
Inundated with dark chocolate . . . .
These are **floods** I wouldn't hate.

I don't mind being inun*dated* with *dates*.

Now you:

_____

_____

_____

_____

_____

Inure

(verb) "In-YOOR"

When you've **adjusted to pain**,
When your **resistance has grown**,
Then you're **inured**.
You're **toughened up**. You're in the zone.

You **inure** to the cold,
And you **inure** to getting old
And to people on your case—
On your back and **inure** face.

You become *inure*d when people are always *in
yer* face.
Oy.

Now you:

_____

_____

_____

_____

_____

Invective

(noun) "In-VEK-tiv"

It's a **nasty** and **raspy** and **biting attack**.
It's a **rant**, it's a **lash**, it's **abuse**.
Like the slandering on PerezHilton.com
Where they dish the celebrity juice.
Invectives can be very funny
Or just angry and bitter and foul.
If the latter, they might seem infective;
If the former, they just make me howl.

REMEMBER THIS:

An angry invective can be infective.

Now you:

_____

_____

_____

_____

_____

Inveterate

(adj) "In-VET-er-it"

Inveterate's **habitual**.
It's **something that's ingrained**,
My parents **drilled** good table manners
Deep into my brain
(**Inveterately**, I complained).

If you were a soldier from the South,
I'll bet it was **inveterate**
To stand up and salute the flag
That showed you were confederate.

REMEMBER THIS:

In the South it was inveterate to be
    confederate.

Now you:

_____

_____

_____

_____

_____

Irksome

(adj) "ERK-sum"

Irksome people **irritate**,
So much you end up shouting.
The Olsen twins, **they bug me**
With that **irksome**, poser pouting.

I'm sure you know a girl
Who thinks she's cute and kind of quirky
While everybody else
Just thinks she's **bothersome** and **irky**.

Irksome people irk some people.

Now you:

_____

_____

_____

_____

_____

Jocular

(adj) "JOK-yoo-ler"

Jocular people **mock** and **make jokes**.
I feel **jocular**
Whenever I see people smoke.
That is,
If I don't feel like whacking their heads.
Nothing **funny**
About taking the fast track to dead.

If you're jocular, you're a joker.

Now you:

_____

_____

_____

_____

_____

Judicious

(adj) "Joo-DISH-us"

Judge Judy is **judicious**.
She must be **fair and wise**—
Showing soundest judgment—
Although she might despise
All those goofballs and their lies.

Judicious—like a judge.

Now you:

_____
_____
_____
_____
_____

Keepsake

(noun) "KEEP-sake"

A **keepsake** is like a **memento**,
A **token**, or a **souvenir**.
It might be your favorite guitar pick
Or the cap from your first bottled beer.

It's simply a **thing you hold onto**,
So it might be a bracelet you wear,
Or a ticket from when you saw Kanye,
Or that blue poodle thing from the fair.

A _keepsake_: something you _keep_ for memory's _sake_.

Now you:

_____
_____
_____
_____
_____

K

Knavery

(noun) "NAVE-er-ee"

Dishonest dealing and **trickery**.
There you have it: **knavery**.
As we all know, there was plenty of this
During the horrible era of slavery.

There was a lot of knavery during slavery.

Now you:

_____

_____

_____

_____

_____

Knoll

(noun) "NOLE"

It's a **small**, **rounded hill**.
Whoopdeedoo!
What a thrill.
Don't bother to ski it
Or try it snowboarding.
A **little** ole **knoll**
Wouldn't be too rewarding.

You can just roll down a knoll.

Now you:

_____

_____

_____

_____

_____

Lackadaisical

(adj) "Lak-uh-DAYZ-ih-kul"

Lazy,
Lethargic,
And so **indolent**.
Did I mention **slacker**?
Well, that's what I meant.

I'm bound to be quite
Lackadaisical
When I'm whacked from no sleep
Or I'm really full.

Lackadaisical=slackadaisical.

Now you:

_____

_____

_____

_____

_____

Lackluster

(adj) "LAK-lus-ter"

Something **lackluster** is **lifeless** and **dull**.
Fat Albert felt **lackluster**
'Cause he was full.

If your charm on that very first date
Is **lackluster**
Don't plan on taking her out again, Buster.

Something lackluster lacks luster.

Now you:

_____

_____

_____

_____

L

Languid

(adj) "LANG-gwid"

Languid just means **sluggish**;
It means something's **getting weak**.
I think you know how **languidly**
Some people like to speak:
"I'm like," "I'm all," "Yeah, totally."
I can't describe the anguish
An English teacher feels
As our language starts to **languish**.

Don't let your *lang*uage be *lang*uid.

Now you:

_____

_____

_____

_____

_____

Laud

(verb) "LAWD"

Are you kidding . . . **laud**?
You want to learn **laud**?
It's so freaking simple,
Oh my gawd.
Okay, whatever . . .
It's to **flatter**, to **praise**.
It's a kind and gracious tradition.
You can see the word here
In **applause** and **applaud**.
Can we get to some *real* definitions?

To laud is to applaud.

Now you:

_____

_____

_____

_____

_____

Lethargic

(adj) "Leh-THAR-jik"

You're **draggy** and **sluggish**
And **lazy** and **blah**.
When my dog is **lethargic**,
He won't lift a paw.

I'll help you remember this one with a lisp.
You know, when you talk
But your S's aren't crisp?
When you're **lethargic**
Or feeling all thtrethed,
You **have much leth energy**;
Go get thum retht.

REMEMBER THIS:

I'm lethargic—that'th why I have leth energy than I youthed to.

Now you:

_____

_____

_____

_____

_____

Libel

(noun) "LY-bul"

To **make damaging statements** . . .
To do it **in writing** . . .
That we call **libel**,
And there starts the fighting.

But what if the **damaging statement**
Is true,
Like "Howard Stern truly belongs in a zoo"?
If you believe
That your statement is true and has merit,
Take out your pen,
Write the statement, and share it.
Ugly or not, **write** the truth, so I say.
Libel or not, it's the 'merican way.

REMEMBER THIS:

If you commit _libel_, you're _liable_ to be sued.

Now you:

_____

_____

_____

_____

_____

L

Libertine

(noun) "LIB-er-teen"

It's when people are
Free from restrictions
And tend to **do just as they please**.
Their **morals are few**,
And they're **sexually free**—
They **take quite a few liberties**.

Do you know anybody who's like this?
You might think I'm just being mean,
But isn't bizarre Michael Jackson
A notorious old **libertine**?

REMEMBER THIS:

A *libertine* takes moral *liberties*.

Now you:

_____
_____
_____
_____
_____

Lilliputian

(adj) "Lil-ih-PYOO-shun"

If you read *Gulliver's Travels*
Then you know the deal:
Lilliputian is **tiny**. I'm talking, *for real*.
Lilliputians were people
Near six inches tall
Who tied up old Gulliver—
Legs, arms, and all.
So, think **really small**—think of this:
Lillipuny;
That is,
If you don't think the word is too loony.

If you were a writer how cool would it be
If your make-believe word
Made the dictionary?

REMEMBER THIS:

Lilli*pu*tian is *puny*—*Lillipuny*.

Now you:

_____
_____
_____
_____
_____

Lionize

(verb) "LY-un-ize"

Treat someone **like a celebrity**
And that's **worshipping**. That's **lionizing**.
Some actors pretend they don't like it,
But they're actors, so that's not surprising.

Angelina Jolie, that poor baby . . .
She can't even use a disguise
'Cause there really is no camouflaging
That mouth and those great lion eyes.

REMEMBER THIS:

We lionize Angelina and her lion eyes.

Now you:

_____

_____

_____

_____

Loquacious

(adj) "Loe-QUAY-shus"

It's **talkative**, **wordy**, and **yakky**.
It's **voluble**, **blabby**, and **chatty**.
Loquaciousy types drive me loco;
When they just **won't shut up**,
I go batty.

Julia Roberts called
Herself **loquacious**
At the Oscars in front of the world.
But I swear she pronounced it
"Lo-quish-iss."
I laughed 'til I practically hurled.

REMEMBER THIS:

Loquacious people make me loco.

Now you:

_____

_____

_____

_____

L

Lugubrious

(adj) "Luh-GOOB-ree-us"

Mournful and **dismal** and **gloomy**—
That's what **lugubrious** means.
You're **dreary** and **draggy** and **mopey**.
Maybe you need some caffeine.

That precious old donkey named Eeyore—
A **lugubrious** fellow he is.
Always **lugging his problems** behind him;
He's the **cloudiest guy** in showbiz.

REMEMBER THIS:

*Lug*ubrious: always *lugg*ing your problems around.

Now you:

_____

_____

_____

_____

_____

Lurid

(adj) "LOOR-id"

This word can mean **shocking** and **vivid**,
And it also means **gruesome**, **revolting**.
When you see something **lurid**
In life or on screen,
You might find it **creepy** and **jolting**.
Lurid events can be awful,
But we all must be **lurid** within
'Cause we stare at dead skunks
And at staggering drunks;
Lurid things lure us right in.

REMEMBER THIS:

*Lur*id things *lure* us.

Now you:

_____

_____

_____

_____

_____

Maelstrom

(noun) "MALE-strum"

It's a **restless**, **disordered**,
And **chaotic state**.
It's when **things have gone nuts**
And the world is **irate**.
It sounds like a ***mail storm***,
So just picture this:
When someone goes postal,
A **maelstrom** exists.

If you go postal, you cause a *mail storm*,
a *maelstrom*.

Now you:

_____

_____

_____

_____

_____

Malapropism

(noun) "MAL-uh-prop-izm"

This is **when**
Somebody messes up words.
She'll **replace what she means**
With some word that she's heard.
Some are so **funny**,
They'll make your heart skip,
Like "These are *pimentos*
I saved from my trip."

George Dubya said plenty
That made the press smile,
Like "Terrorists won't hold this nation
Hostile"!
Vice President Quayle malapropped . . .
It was wild! He said,
"Let's have more *bondage*
Between Mom and child!"

Mala*prop*isms are im*prop*er speech.

Now you:

_____

_____

_____

_____

_____

M

Malinger
(verb) "Muh-LING-er"

This word is pretty specific.
It means that you **sleaze out of work**
By **pretending you're sick**.
It's a really old trick.
Don't be a **malingering** jerk.

REMEMBER THIS:

You malinger so you won't have to lift a finger.

Now you:

_____

_____

_____

_____

_____

Mawkish
(adj) "MAWK-ish"

Mawkish young lovers
Are **too sentimental**;
Their hearts are all **mushy** and raw.
Some are so **mawkish**
They start being stalkish
And stretching the bounds of the law.

Romeo's friends got together to tease him.
They ribbed and they razzed
And they mocked
'Cause that poor **mawkish** lad
Really had it quite bad;
He thought all his girlie friends rocked.

REMEMBER THIS:

Romeo was *mock*ed for being *mawk*ish.

Now you:

_____

_____

_____

_____

_____

Melancholy

(adj) "MEL-in-kol-ee"

You had to see this one coming
Because "collie" is there in the word;
This clue has to be about Lassie
Despite that it's lame and absurd.
Lassie was quite the good actress,
And most of the time she was jolly,
But the day they replaced her
With Felix the Cat
She was **sad**,
Which just means **melancholy**.

After Lassie was fired, she was a melancholy collie.

Now you:

_____

_____

_____

_____

_____

Meticulous

(adj) "Meh-TIK-yoo-less"

Fussy, **finicky**, **careful of details**—
That describes a person
Who's **meticulous**.
There are lots of girls
Who get this way about their nails,
So much so they really seem ridiculous.

Meticulous: so fussy it's ridiculous.

Now you:

_____

_____

_____

_____

_____

M

Mettle

(noun) "MET-el"

It's **courage** and **fortitude**,
Valor and **nerve**.
Soldiers with **mettle**
Will sign up and serve.
You know which two kids
Showed a truckload of **mettle**?
Those clever young rejects
Named Hansel and Gretel.

REMEMBER THIS:

The soldier showed so much mettle, they gave
her a medal.

Now you:

_____

_____

_____

_____

_____

Miasma

(noun) "My-AZZ-muh"

Miasma means **pollution**
Or a **toxic atmosphere**,
Smog or **vapor**, maybe even **smoke**.
In the crowded cities
Where **the air just isn't clear**,
My asthma rages, and I want to choke.

REMEMBER THIS:

Miasma really messes with _my asthma_.

Now you:

_____

_____

_____

_____

_____

Misconstrue

(verb) "Mis-kun-STROO"

So you told your best friend
That her boyfriend is hot,
And now your old friendship is in a big knot
'Cause she thinks you want him;
She's up for combat.
But the fact is,
You'd never do something like that.
She **misconstrued**
What you meant when you said it.
She **misunderstood**
Or **misjudged** or **misread** it.
Try to lie low;
For the moment you're screwed.
Doesn't it suck
When you've been **misconstrued**?

When you *miscons*true* you *miss* what's *true*.

Now you:

_____

_____

_____

_____

_____

Mitigate

(verb) "MIT-ih-gate"

To **lessen the force or intensity**,
To **ease** or to **mellow the pain**.
The brush fires
That spread through the Southland
Were soon **mitigated** by rain.

My dad was a big baseball player
(Yet I never saw him chew and spit).
When I said, "Catching baseballs
Is hurting my hands!"
He said, "**Mitigate** that with a mitt."

A baseball *mitt mit*igates the pain.

Now you:

_____

_____

_____

_____

M

Moony

(adj) "MOON-ee"

Daydreamy, **faraway**, **silly in mood**.
If someone looks **moony**, try not to intrude.
Women become kind of **silly** and **moony**
Whenever they get around guys
Like George Clooney.

Moony: When your mood seems to be affected by the moon.

Now you:

_____
_____
_____
_____
_____

Moot

(adj) "MOOT"

The most common meanings
I know for this one are:
Not relevant, **useless**,
And kind of **undone**.
Whenever you think
That an argument's **moot**,
You might say it's **pointless**,
No longer bears fruit.
Don't mispronounce it
And say the point's "mute,"
Or I'll laugh, pat your head, and say,
"Isn't she cute?"

If a point is moot, people don't give a hoot.

Now you:

_____
_____
_____
_____
_____

Mordant

(adj) "MOR-dent"

Well giddyup, yo.
Now we're talking my speed.
It's **nasty**, **sarcastic**.
What morda you need?
Not much I like better,
I have to admit,
Than a guy with a wink
And a **dark**, **mordant** wit.

I'm *mordan*t a lot *more dan* my mother
would like.
Help.

Now you:

_____

_____

_____

_____

_____

Multifarious

(adj) "Mul-tih-FARE-ee-us"

It's **mixed**, **diverse**, **assorted**,
So let's make this clue quick.
Multifarious rhymes with **various**.
That oughta make the word stick.

Multifarious is various.

Now you:

_____

_____

_____

_____

_____

M

Mundane

(adj) "Mun-DANE"

Ordinary, **practical**—that's **mundane**.
Day after day, just **average** and **plain**.
Many facts that are **mundane**
Embed into a teenaged brain.

If days of the week have attitude—
Like Fridays are insane,
And Sundays are kind of sleepy,
Then Monday is **mundane**.

Monday is plain and *munda*ne.

Now you:

_____

_____

_____

_____

_____

Munificent

(adj) "Myoo-NIF-ih-sent"

It means **very generous**.
That's what it means.
Munificently,
Santa brought me Guess jeans.

Bill Gates could be called
A **munificent** guy.
Well, it helps to be loaded.
I'm not gonna lie.

It's magnificent to be munificent.

Now you:

_____

_____

_____

_____

_____

Muse

(verb) "MYOOZE"

It's to **think** and to **daydream**,
To **ponder**, to **gaze**.
When you sit and you **muse**,
You might look in a daze.
Some people think that to sit and to **muse**
Is a lazy excuse to just mentally snooze,
But when talented people
Are **musing** and smirking,
The truth of the deal is
They're actually working.

REMEMBER THIS:

The day I was musing my boss said,
  "No snoozing!"

Now you:

_____

_____

_____

_____

_____

Nadir

(noun) "NAY-der"

It's your **lowest point**,
Your **darkest day**,
The **bottom of your barrel**.
Your grades have hit their **nadir**?
You had better fix that peril.

Nate had lots of cruddy jobs,
But he sure hit his **nadir**
That summer spent at Chuck E. Cheese
As garbage guy and waiter.

REMEMBER THIS:

Nate was at his nadir as a Chuck E. Cheese
  waiter.

Now you:

_____

_____

_____

_____

_____

N

Narcissist

(noun) "NAR-sis-ist"

A **narcissist** is **in love with himself**,
And I don't mean in a good way.
He's **vain** and **stuck up** and **self
centered**.
He might stare in the mirror all day.

In mythology, Narcissus sat by the river—
He'd fallen for his own reflection.
If you asked me I'd say
That was looking for love
In a totally stupid direction.

REMEMBER THIS:

Narcissist: From Narcissus, the mythological
boy who fell in love with his reflection.

Now you:

_____

_____

_____

_____

Nascent

(adj) "NAY-sent"

Something that's **nascent**
Is **newborn** or **young**.
It's only **just come to exist**.
I'll link it to NASA, the Space Program.
This is stupid, but I can't resist.
This isn't the easiest word in the world . . .
You pronounce the word
NAS-ent _or_ NAY-sent,
So think of it this way:
When NASA was young,
No one had traveled in spacent.
Help.

REMEMBER THIS:

When NASA was nascent, there was no travel
in spacent.

Now you:

_____

_____

_____

_____

_____

Nebulous

(adj) "NEB-yoo-less"

It's **cloudy** and **vague**
And **kind of unclear**.
You've heard of a nebula, right?
It's the **vapory** mist
Where a star will appear—
A **nebulous fuzz** in the night.

Nebulous people make me kind of crazy;
I hate it when stories are **murky** and **hazy**.
And **nebulous** arguments never convince;
Without the specifics, I yawn or I wince.

REMEMBER THIS:

Nebulous=vague, cloudy, like a nebula.

Now you:

Necessitate

(verb) "Neh-SESS-ih-tate"

To **make necessary**. **Compel** or **oblige**.
Life **necessitates things that you need**.
Food and water, you bet,
But not a Learjet;
At that point it's just about greed.
But if crazy fans
Chase you through airports,
Then a jet may be **necessitated**.
It sounds as if fame
Is a troublesome game;
Being drooled on is way overrated.

REMEMBER THIS:

*Necess*itate is to make *necess*ary.

Now you:

Nefarious

(adj) "Neh-FARE-ee-us"

Heinous and **evil** and **villainous** types
Are **awful** and **cruel** and **nefarious**.
In nightmares they show up
And haunt us and stalk us,
And sometimes they might even bury us.

So **nefarious** creatures
Will threaten and scare.
Try to remember this: *never* and *fair*.

REMEMBER THIS:

If he's ne*farious*, he's never *fair* to *us*.

Now you:

_____

_____

_____

_____

_____

Neophyte

(noun) "NEE-oe-fite"

In the popular movie, *The Matrix*
Neo is **new to the game**,
And since **neophyte** means a **beginner**,
I'll bet that's how they chose his name.

REMEMBER THIS:

Neophyte—Neo was new to the fight.

Now you:

_____

_____

_____

_____

Nondescript

(adj) "Non-dih-SKRIPT"

It's **not much to say about** someone,
When he's **of no particular kind**.
Nondescript people are **nebulous** . . .
Difficult to be defined.

That guy on the Calvin Klein billboard . . .
He handsome and totally ripped,
But what else does anyone say about him?
Not much,
So he's called **nondescript**.

REMEMBER THIS:

Nondescript=not worthy of much *description.*

Now you:

_____
_____
_____
_____
_____

Noxious

(adj) "NOK-shus"

Noxious fumes are **poisonous**
And **lethal** and **gross**.
Car exhaust and sewage plants—
Those gag me the most.

People can be **noxious**,
Like DJs on radio.
That's why I take my iPod
Nearly everywhere I go.

REMEMBER THIS:

*Nox*ious—it's where *tox*ic meets ob*nox*ious.

Now you:

_____
_____
_____
_____
_____

N

Obfuscate

(verb) "OB-fuh-skate"

I've held back 'til now,
But here I come . . .
I do this thing that's kind of dumb:
I make up words (I must reveal),
And then I use them like they're real.
So here we go:
To **obfuscate** is trying to **confusiate**,
Perplex or **cloud**, **mess with my head**—
Confusiate!
Just like I said.

REMEMBER THIS:

If you're obfuscated, you're confusiated.

Now you:

_____
_____
_____
_____
_____

Obsequious

(adj) "Ub-SEE-qwee-us"

I love this word.
It means you're **a suck up**,
A **fawning cajoler**.
Makes me want to chuck up.

An **obsequious** girl
Is a **major butt kisser**.
When she finally leaves,
You really don't miss her.

REMEMBER THIS:

Ob*sequ*ious people *seek* your approval.

Now you:

_____
_____
_____
_____
_____

Obtuse

(adj) "Ob-TOOSE"

Very slow to get the point
Is a **dopey, obtuse** fellow.
I'd compare his sharpness
To a gushy, warm marshmallow.

My mom pretends to be **obtuse** . . .
Can't imagine what I mean . . .
When I say I need two hundred bucks
For wicked skinny jeans.

Ob*tuse*=not *too* smart.

Now you:

_____

_____

_____

_____

_____

Odious

(adj) "OE-dee-us"

Hateful, detestable, heinous, and **mean**.
Odious scenes fill the big movie screens.
And what of rap music?
Sure, some is melodious,
But too many artists are tacky and **odious**.

Hey, I have a clue . . .
Not a bad one, I think.
Think "odorous";
Odious actions stink.

Odious—think odorous. Odious behavior stinks.

Now you:

_____

_____

_____

_____

_____

Officious

(adj) "Uh-FISH-us"

Have you ever had an office job?
I doubt it, but you might.
Officious people work there,
And they're great for office fights.
They **push opinions down your throat**.
They **meddle, interfere**.
Should I get an office job?
No thanks. I'll stay right here
In my jammies with a beer.

Of*ficious* people *fish* around in your business.

Now you:

_____

_____

_____

_____

_____

Olfactory

(adj) "Ole-FAK-tor-ee"

Olfactory pertains
To **your sense of smell**.
It has something to do with your **nose**.
My **olfactories** say you were smoking;
I can **smell** it all over your clothes.
So now you just **reek** like a factory.
That's what your cigarettes do:
They offend my precious **olfactories**.
Goody for cool, smoking you.

My *olfactories* tell me that he smells like an *old factory*.

Now you:

_____

_____

_____

_____

_____

Opine

(verb) "Oe-PINE"

Do you know that chatty, big-mouthed kid
Who **always says what he thinks**
And doesn't care that people stare
Or say that his judgment stinks?
He **voices his opinions**,
Which means that he **opines**.
I love to hear **opinions**,
Especially when they're mine.

REMEMBER THIS:

*Opin*ing is giving your *opin*ion.

Now you:

_____

_____

_____

_____

_____

Ostensible

(adj) "Aw-STENS-ih-bul"

**When something appears
To be one way**,
But in fact that's **not really the case**,
That's **ostensible** and **inauthentic**,
Like a big **phony** smile on your face.

All that air brushing in magazines
Is a game that's really **ostensible**.
Those people appear to be flawless,
But glossed over is really not sensible.

REMEMBER THIS:

*Ost*ensible is kind of *glossed*ensible.

Now you:

_____

_____

_____

_____

_____

Ostentatious

(adj) "Os-ten-TAY-shus"

Ostentatious tells of those
Who **try to dazzle or impress**
With their cars and with their houses,
With their style of speech and dress.

Austin Powers is a helpful link
To learning **ostentatious**;
He's **overdone** and **showy**
While he's being so flirtatious.

Austin Powers is *osten*tatious.

Now you:

_____

_____

_____

_____

_____

Ostracize

(verb) "OS-truh-size"

Shut out of the group
And **told to hit the road**.
If you're **ostracized**, you just might need to
Find a new zip code.

Think about an ostrich . . .
He's a bird who never flies,
So the other birds **exclude** him.
They mock and **ostracize**.

The *ostr*ich was *ostr*acized.

Now you:

_____

_____

_____

_____

_____

Palatial

(adj) "Puh-LAY-shul"

Palatial's **like a palace**—
A home **with lots of space**.
If your house is called **palatial**,
You can skate across the place.

In West Egg, on Long Island,
Jay Gatsby's **mansion** stood.
He threw **palatial** parties.
The biggest in the hood.

*Pala*tial=resembling a *pala*ce.

Now you:

_____

_____

_____

_____

_____

Palaver

(verb) "Pu-LA-ver"

It's **yakking** and it's **babbling**.
It's **simple**, **idle chatter**.
You **palaver** with your pals,
Talking trash that doesn't matter.

You *pala*ver with your *pal*s.

Now you:

_____

_____

_____

_____

_____

Palliate

(verb) "PAL-ee-ate"

Palliate means to **alleviate**,
To **soothe**, or to **lessen the pain**.
Your pals **palliate**
If you've had a crap date;
They don't care if you whine and complain.

My brother was quite the big eater,
And he begged Pepto Bismol to **palliate**
The gurgling storm in his stomach
From that huge
Brownie sundae royale he ate.

Your *pals* help *pal*liate your pain.

Now you:

_____

_____

_____

_____

_____

Pallid

(adj) "PAL-id"

It's **pale** and **washed out**,
Kinda **sickly** and **light**.
You know who was **pallid**?
That silly Snow White.
Her fairy godmother told Snow, "Get a life.
Stop sitting and hoping
To be some guy's wife.
Another thing,
Know why you're skinny and **pallid**?
'Cause all that you eat
Is that cheap iceberg salad."

*Pall*id is *pal*e.

Now you:

_____

_____

_____

_____

_____

Palpable

(adj) "PALP-uh-bul"

You can **touch** or **see**
Something that's **palpable**;
It's **plain** as the race on your face.
If the tension somewhere is just **palpable**,
I'd pay to get out of that place.

So heart palpitations are **palpable**;
Your heart goes so wild you **perceive it**.
David Beckham
Makes girls' heartbeats **palpable**.
The screaming?
You wouldn't believe it.

REMEMBER THIS:

Heart *palp*itations are *palp*able.

Now you:

_____

_____

_____

_____

_____

Paltry

(noun) "PAL-tree"

It's **insignificant, worthless**.
A **paltry** amount is **lame**.
This word made me think about Gwyneth,
Just because of the Paltrow name.
But I don't think of her as **paltry**,
So I'll write the clue in reverse.
I'll bet that Gwyneth Paltrow
Keeps **unpaltry** amounts in her purse.
(*Okay . . . whatever . . . so "unpaltry" isn't
a word.*)

REMEMBER THIS:

What's in Gwyneth Paltrow's purse is *not* paltry.

Now you:

_____

_____

_____

_____

_____

Parsimony

(noun) "PAR-sih-mone-ee"

It's **extremely frugal**.
Now, I'm talking **cheap**.
When the dinner check comes,
This guy won't make a peep.
Parsimonious people
Won't part with their money.
A **cheapskate** blind date?
Girl, that's not even funny.

REMEMBER THIS:

Parsimony: You won't *part* with your *money*.

Now you:

_____

_____

_____

_____

_____

Pedestrian

(adj) "Peh-DEST-ree-in"

Pedestrian, the noun, means
Someone who walks.
As an adjective, it's **dull** and **plain**.
If your writing is sounding **pedestrian**,
Wake up and start using your brain.

Remember when Mom would say
"WALK" through a store?
But running was so much more fun.
It's the same with your writing:
Revise a **dull** draft,
And make the **pedestrian** run.

REMEMBER THIS:

Pedestrian talk is like a slow, boring walk.

Now you:

_____

_____

_____

_____

_____

Penury

(noun) "PEN-yuh-ree"

It's **extreme poverty**.
Little Oliver Twist
Knew such bad **penury**,
He could barely exist.

If you are this **poor**,
You **don't have a spare penny**.
Just like in *South Park*—
That describes little Kenny.

If you live in *pen*ury, you can't spare a *pen*ny.

Now you:

_____

_____

_____

_____

_____

Perfunctory

(adj) "Per-FUNK-ter-ee"

Perfunctory "effort" is **careless**.
I'm guessing that no one likes that.
If your hairdresser's work was **perfunctory**,
You're probably wearing a hat.

I always attempt to be careful and sure
Whenever I'm taking a test,
But when I am told,
"Go and clean up your room!"
My effort's **perfunctory** at best.

If your studying was **perfunct-ory**
It's likely that you flunked-ory.
Help.

*Perfunc*tory: Like your *perfor*mance is in a *funk*.

Now you:

_____

_____

_____

_____

_____

Peripatetic
(noun) "Pare-ih-puh-TET-ik"

It's **someone who walks**
And **who travels about**;
And trust me, I mean *quite a lot*.
This person is kind of a **wanderer**.
A big lazy blob he is not. .
A peripatetic is so energetic.
A peripatetic is so energetic.
No, I don't think that you're stupid or thick;
I really just want the word's meaning
To stick.

REMEMBER THIS:

A peripatetic is so energetic.

Now you:

_____
_____
_____
_____
_____

Pernicious
(adj) "Per-NIH-shus"

Pernicious things **cause harm**.
Pernicious people **lead to ruin**,
So if you keep **pernicious** friends,
I ask: *what* are you chewin?

Hey, if you found a genie
Who would grant you thirty wishes,
Wouldn't that just suck if
He turned out to be **pernicious**?

REMEMBER THIS:

Pernicious is vicious.

Now you:

_____
_____
_____
_____
_____

Perpetuate

(verb) "Per-PECH-oo-ate"

It means to **make long lasting**.
It means to **keep it going**.
I swear that up in Maine
The gods **perpetuate** the snowing.

Even if your cat is one of those
Who's always shedding,
Be a good pet owner
And **perpetuate** the petting.

Per*pet*uate *pet*ting your *pet*.

Now you:

_____

_____

_____

_____

_____

P

Perspicacious

(adj) "Pers-pih-KAY-shus"

Perceptive with **insight**
And **keen understanding**,
Our principal is **perspicacious**.
She **knows** which kids
Are bugging the teachers
By being all rude and loquacious.
She most **perspicaciously**
Watches the halls,
She **can spot** any vandal or liar.
She's so good that some kids believe
She's a witch,
And when she walks by, they perspire.

*Pers*picacious people are *perc*eptive.

Now you:

_____

_____

_____

_____

_____

Perverse

(adj) "Per-VERSE"

In ninth grade
I knew of this small group of guys—
The biggest perverts in our school.
They spied in the girls' locker room
Every day
Thinking they were all sneaky and cool.
These guys were **perverse**;
They were **headstrong** and **naughty**,
Disobedient, **stubborn**, and **bad**.
Our vice principal caught 'em,
And then the guy brought 'em
To 'fess up in front of our dads.
And get this: those wicked, **perverse**
Little geeks
Cleaned the girls' locker room
For the next twenty weeks.

REMEMBER THIS:

*Perv*erted people are *perv*erse.

Now you:

_____

_____

_____

_____

_____

Petulant

(adj) "PECH-oo-lent"

It's **quickly annoyed** and **easily grouchy**,
With **irritability** factor.
The big gossip mongers of Hollywood say
Russell Crowe is a **petulant** actor.
The press and the public
Get so **on his nerves**
That sometimes he will take a swing.
Hey, if had those dopes in my face,
I might do the very same thing.

REMEMBER THIS:

Don't try to *pet* a *pet*ulant crow.

Now you:

_____

_____

_____

_____

_____

Philanderer

(noun) "Fih-LAN-der-er"

This is a **guy who gets around**.
He's a big old **womanizer**,
And then he complains
That he can't find love.
I'm not a big sympathizer.

A **philanderer** loves when he's **flirting**.
He's a **cruiser**—all charming and slick.
But **philandering** must be exhausting . . .
Always working to *land* a new chick.

A phi*lander*er wants to *land her.*

Now you:

_____

_____

_____

_____

_____

Philistine

(noun) "FIL-ih-stine"

Some are **indifferent or hostile to art**;
They're **lacking in culture**
But think they're so smart.
They're **philistines**, and they have
Plain, common taste.
Don't send caviar;
That would be a big waste.

So what if we link the word to Dr. Phil?
Let's pay him a compliment,
Give him a thrill:
He loves the ballet and to wine and to dine
Because he is not a big, dumb **philistine**.

Dr. Phil *isn't* a philistine.
Or if he is, he'd better step it up by the time this book comes out.

Now you:

_____

_____

_____

_____

_____

Pilfer, Pillage, Plunder
(verbs) "PIL-fer" "PILL-ij" "PLUN-der"

Say these three words just like Dorothy
Chanting "Lions and Tigers and Bears"
(oh my).
Chant "**Pilfer** and **Pillage** and **Plunder**,"
(oh my)
And then count all the jittery stares.

They all mean **to steal**,
Although **pilfer**
Means to **steal just a little amount**,
While the other two mean **bigger rip-offs**,
Like to strip Oprah's whole bank account.

REMEMBER THIS:

If you pilfer or plunder or pillage,
   You're ripping things off from the village.

Now you:

_____

_____

_____

_____

_____

Placid
(adj) "PLA-sid"

It's **peaceful** and **tranquil**.
It's **calm** and it's **quiet**.
If I find a nice house on Lake Placid,
I'll buy it.

If you happen to like
When your stomach is **placid**,
Lay off spicy foods;
They produce gastric acid.

REMEMBER THIS:

To keep your stomach pl*acid*, avoid the *acid*.

Now you:

_____

_____

_____

_____

_____

Plaintive

(adj) "PLANE-tiv"

There once was a lonely coyote
(Sounds like a folksy old tale).
He was **sad**, he was **low**,
He was **plaintive**,
So he tipped his poor head back to wail.

It ain't easy to be a coyote—
You eat cute, furry creatures all day . . .
Which can make a guy kind of unpopular.
What am I trying to say?
That **lonely** and **sad** bunny eater
(Who'd prefer a wild bash with champagne)
Roamed day and night, **melancholy**.
Life was **plaintively** plain on the plain.

REMEMBER THIS:

The coyote is *plain*tive out on the *plain*s.

Now you:

_____

_____

_____

_____

_____

Platitude

(noun) "PLAT-ih-tood"

Platitudes are **stale expressions**.
Using them is like
A broken leg in my profession.
"Everything will be okay."
"He's in a better place."
"The message is as clear
As that big nose upon your face."
Do your best to avoid **boring platitudes**
'Cause otherwise the world will find you
Dull and flatitude.

REMEMBER THIS:

Platitudes are flatitude.

Now you:

_____

_____

_____

_____

_____

Porcine

(adj) "PORE-sine"

Canine is a word that refers to dogs,
And murine—to rodents, like rats.
Equine for horses and lupine for wolves
And feline refers to my cat.

And here comes my point:
Porcine is for **pigs**.
Hey, why doesn't figurine refer to figs?

If you hear that your date called you
Sweet but **porcine**,"
Grab your silk purse and
Abandon the **swine**.

*Porc*ine creatures give us *pork*.

Now you:

_____

_____

_____

_____

_____

Praxis

(noun) "PRAX-iss"

Praxis: it simply means **practice** or **use**,
Like *in practice* and not just *in theory*.
If someone is pitching a theory, no proof . . .
You oughta be just a bit leery.
And **praxis** *sounds* like the word **practice**,
So another word's totally easy.
Remember that **praxis** makes perfect!
(*Omigod that was totally cheesy.*)

Praxis is something put into practice.

Now you:

_____

_____

_____

_____

_____

Precarious

(adj) "Prih-KARE-ee-us"

Dangerous, unstable,
And it **could mean insecure.**
Precarious explorers
Like to search where they're **unsure.**
Imagine you go hiking
In **precarious** conditions;
You might slip
And find yourself in tangled-up positions
(And then examined by physicians).

Pre*cari*ous people aren't very *care*ful.

Now you:

_____
_____
_____
_____
_____

Precedent

(noun) "PRESS-ih-dent"

It's an **example** or **case**
That came before
And **serves as a model.**
Is this one a bore?
See there: **precede,**
Which means **go before?**
The thrill of this rhyme
Might just lead me to snore.

Okay, how 'bout this:
What of George Washington?
You have to admit,
That guy cracked a homerun.
He meant what he said,
And he said what he meant.
As president he set a mean **precedent.**

George Washington set a *precedent* for how to be *president.*

Now you:

_____
_____
_____
_____
_____

Prevaricate

(verb) "Prih-VARE-ih-kate"

If you despise
People's **fiction** and **lies**,
It sounds like you hate
When they **prevaricate**.

Next time your guy looks you in the eye
And tells a fat **lie**, give this one a try:
"I'm sorry Bud, but I don't date
A joker who **prevaricates**.
Now hit the road and have a very
Nice time with your dictionary."
*(Get it? He doesn't know what prevaricate
means, so he has to look it up. Get it? Oh,
never mind.)*

REMEMBER THIS:

Prevarication prevents verification.

Now you:

_____

_____

_____

_____

_____

Privation

(noun) "Pry-VAY-shun"

Again the English language has me
bothered and tense—
Here's another that doesn't make sense:
Privation means you **lack what you need**.
You're somewhat **deprived**
(Does that prefix *not* mislead?).

Privation/deprivation . . .
Both words link to **deprived**,
Just like flammable/inflammable . . .
This language is contrived!!

REMEMBER THIS:

Privation and deprivation mean the same!!
  Whatever!!

Now you:

_____

_____

_____

_____

_____

Procure

(verb) "Proe-KYER"

It's to **get**, to **obtain** . . .
And **through effort**.
Go out and **procure** a good job.
It's about time you start making money,
So you won't be a freeloading slob.

Think about medical research . . .
You can follow me here, I am sure:
Think of people who stamp out diseases.
They work at **procuring** a cure.

REMEMBER THIS:

Researchers try to pro*cure* a *cure*.

Now you:

Prodigy

(noun) "PROD-ih-jee"

A **child of unusual talent**, you see,
Is considered a **genius** or great **prodigy**.

Did you hear of that three-year-old kid
From Ukraine
Who can drive, play piano,
And pilot a plane?
Me neither.
I just made it up. I'm a jerk.
But I thought that a crazy example
Would work.
Come on, relax. You have to agree—
That kid would be an intense **prodigy**.

REMEMBER THIS:

Gee, I'll bet you don't have to *prod* a *prodigy*.

Now you:

Prognosticate

(verb) "Prog-NOS-tih-kate"

It's **predict**, just like a **fortune teller**.
My talent with this stuff is stellar.
If you want to know your **fate**
Call me
And I'll **prognosticate**.

It's like the word **prognosis**
(**Guessing outcome from disease**).
Watch this:
"You have a cold, so I **predict**
That you will sneeze."
Man, I'm good.

*Prognos*ticate=predict, as with a *prognos*is.

Now you:

_____

_____

_____

_____

_____

Prolific

(adj) "Proe-LIF-ik"

You're **producing a lot** of whatever,
So that makes you **prolific**.
It could be music, books, or cupcakes.
In any case—terrific.

I think that I'm pretty **prolific** . . .
Just think of the sleep that I've skipped
While I knocked out this volume of vocab.
Learn 'em, so I don't feel gypped.

*Pro*lific people *pro*duce a lot.

Now you:

_____

_____

_____

_____

_____

Prosaic

(adj) "Proe-ZAY-ik"

This word once confused me.
It means **common** or **dull**,
But I had linked it to *mosaic*...
That tile that's colorful.
So get it straight—don't be like me:
Prosaic=dull
Mosaic=pretty.

Don't let your *prose* be *prosaic*.

Now you:

_____

_____

_____

_____

_____

Proscribe

(verb) "Proe-SCRIBE"

To **proscribe** a thing is to **banish** it,
To **denounce it as harmful** or **wrong**.
Prescribing is kind of the opposite:
"Hey Doc, that prescription's too strong."

In the morning right after the party,
Your headache will make you complain,
So next time *prescribe* ibuprofen,
And ***proscribe***
That cheap, pink champagne.

*Pro*scribe is kind of the opposite of *pre*scribe.

Now you:

_____

_____

_____

_____

_____

Prowess
(noun) "PROW-ess"

Prowess means **bravery**, **valor**, or **skill**.
He conquered in battle
With **prowess** and will.
When Dad displays **prowess**,
Just tell him you're proud.
Pat his bald head,
And yell "DUDE!" really loud.

*Prow*ess makes you feel *prou*d.

Now you:

_____

_____

_____

_____

_____

Prudent
(adj) "PROO-dent"

Sensible, **wise**, and **judicious** . . .
That's what it means to be **prudent**.
The fact that you're sitting here
Reading this book
Implies that you're this kind of student.

A good student is prudent.

Now you:

_____

_____

_____

_____

_____

Pulchritude

(noun) "PULK-rih-tood"

Did you see that lovely film,
Akeelah and the Bee?
This word was the last she had to spell.
It's **beauty**. It means **prettiness**.
But here's the irony:
The word itself is uglier than hell!

Pulchritude sounds clunky,
Maybe even kinda rude.
But anyway, if you are **cute**,
Don't have an attitude.

And if it works to use this word
When speaking of a dude,
Then I must say that Johnny Depp
Has massive **pulchritude**.

REMEMBER THIS:

Don't let pulchr*itude* give you att*itude*.

Now you:

_____

_____

_____

_____

_____

Punctilious

(adj) "Punk-TIL-ee-us"

It's **careful** and **exact**
And **attentive to detail**.
Be **punctilious** on your driver's test,
Or buckle up to fail.

Punctilious people are **punctual**
And tend to be **meticulous**.
That's what you want in a tailor;
Careful tailors tend to stick you less.

REMEMBER THIS:

Punctilious: It's where punctual meets
meticulous.

Now you:

_____

_____

_____

_____

_____

Putrid

(adj) "PYOO-trid"

Putrid is **disgusting**,
In a state of foul decay.
It is **rotten** and it's **smelly**,
Like old garbage, wet and gray.

Okay this clue is **nasty**,
And I might deserve rebuke,
But when I think of **putrid**,
I just think of "make me puke."

REMEMBER THIS:

*Pu*trid things might make you *puke*.

Now you:

_____

_____

_____

_____

_____

Quandary

(noun) "KWON-duh-ree"

When you're in a **quandary**,
You **don't know what to do**.
You're **stuck**. It's a **dilemma** or a **rut**.
"Should I go to college
And work hard for four more years,
Or should I clear the trays at Pizza Hut?"

When I **face dilemmas**
And am feeling kind of **pondery**,
I find it helps to walk around;
A **quandary** makes me wandery.

REMEMBER THIS:

I work through a quandary by being wandery.

Now you:

_____

_____

_____

_____

_____

Querulous
(adj) "KWARE-uh-lus"

A **querulous** girl is a **whiny complainer**.
Don't ask someone grateful like me
To explain her.

Some stupermodels can be **querulous**:
"Don't mess with my makeup!"
They **hassle** and **fuss**.
Their bosses should tell them,
"I couldn't care less!
Put on the damned dress!
No more **querulousness**!"

REMEMBER THIS:

If a model is querulous, I couldn't care-a-less.
ouch.

Now you:

_____
_____
_____
_____
_____

Quixotic
(adj) "Kwix-OT-ik"

Think of the book *Don Quixote*—
You read that old classic one, right?
Don Quixote was **zany**, **impulsive**,
Capricious . . .
Though known as a chivalrous knight.

A **quixotic** guy might be harmless
Or a psycho, a nut, an imposter.
He might try to shoot Ronald Reagan
Just to impress Jodie Foster.
*(Google that crazy incident and get back
to me.)*

REMEMBER THIS:

Quixotic—impulsive like Don *Quixote.*

Now you:

_____
_____
_____
_____
_____

Raconteur

(noun) "Rak-un-TOOR"

I think that I speak for all those in the joint
When I say,
"**Tell your story**, but get to the point!"
A **raconteur** is just a **good storyteller**.
This is a guy who could write a best seller.
When **recounting a tale**,
He is **vivid** and **clear**,
So you don't want to shove
A corkscrew in your ear.

A raconteur *recounts* a story well.

Now you:

_____

_____

_____

_____

_____

Raze

(verb) "RAZE"

This meaning is counter
To what you might think:
It's **tear down**.
"The old building was **razed** in a blink."
So while you raise up, you **raze down**.
Odd enough?
Is vocab annoying?
I just *love* this stuff.

Use a *raz*or to *raz*e your beard.

Now you:

_____

_____

_____

_____

_____

Recidivist

(noun) "Ree-SID-ih-vist"

A **repeat offender** is a **recidivist**.
This guy makes you shake your fist
'Cause you put him away for a **crime**
And then
You let the guy out, and **he does it again**.

Recidivism runs rampant
From LA to Miami.
What's *with* all these jokers?
They must like the orange jammies.

Think "recidi-visitor";
    A recidivist revisits prison.

Now you:

_____
_____
_____
_____
_____

Recuse

(verb) "Rih-KYOOZ"

To **recuse** is to **excuse a judge**
'**Cause he's unfit** to act,
Maybe 'cause he's biased
Or incompetent or wacked.

Judge Ito let the O.J. trial
Become a TV bash.
Some wanted to **recuse** him
Just to stop
The talking trash.

To re*cuse* is to ex*cuse*.

Now you:

_____
_____
_____
_____
_____

R

Redress

(verb) "Ree-DRESS"

To **set a situation right**,
Correct a stupid **mess**,
That's what it means to **redress**.

Picture this:
She sneaked out of the house
Wearing practically nothing.
Her father was not too impressed.
He screamed at his daughter,
"You HAVE to be kidding!
Go right back upstairs and **redress**!"

She redressed the situation when she
re-dressed.

Now you:

_____

_____

_____

_____

_____

Remonstrate

(verb) "Rih-MON-strate"

To **speak out against**, to **object**,
To **protest** . . .
These words describe **remonstrate** best.
If there is an issue
You should **remonstrate**,
Paint up a sign and go on—**demonstrate**.
Show the whole world
What opinions are for.
Stand up and **argue**; **protest** the war
Or some other policy that you oppose.
Will it make a difference?
It might. Who knows?

When I want to r*emonstrate,* I grab a sign and
d*emonstrate.*

Now you:

_____

_____

_____

_____

_____

Repose

(verb) "Rih-POZE"

It's to **feel in a state**
Of extreme relaxation . . .
Tranquil, **at peace**, or **at rest**.
That's how I feel
When I swing on a hammock;
In summer, I'm lazy at best.

Mona Lisa sat still for the artist da Vinci
(I love that sly grin that she chose),
And when she began to get antsy, he said,
"Girl, get up, move around, and re-pose."

REMEMBER THIS:

If you're not reposed, you should re-pose.

Now you:

_____

_____

_____

_____

_____

Repudiate

(verb) "Rih-PYOO-dee-ate"

When telemarketers call you,
Repudiate and **reject**.
Cast them off, **disown** them.
Then call them back, collect.

The word looks just like _reputation_,
And here comes a truth (you might hate it):
If you earn a cheap, low reputation,
I doubt you can **repudiate** it.

REMEMBER THIS:

Good luck _repu_diating a bad _repu_tation.

Now you:

_____

_____

_____

_____

_____

R

Resplendent

(adj) "Ree-SPLEN-dent"

Resplendent is just **beautiful**.
It's **radiant** and **gleaming**.
Cinderella was **resplendent**,
And the prince, at last, was beaming
'Cause Cindy had lost weight,
And now the prince found her hot.
At the last formal gig he said,
"**Resplendent** she's not."
He asked her, "Was it Splenda
That has made you look so **splendid**?"
She said, "Hey beat it, Shorty.
This dumb fairy tale just ended."
Poor little guy was offended.

Re*splend*ent looks *splend*id.

Now you:

_____

_____

_____

_____

_____

Reticent

(adj) "RET-ih-sent"

Reticent kids **don't say much**.
They **don't want to talk**
About feelings and such.
There's really **not much**
That they want to discuss,
But some kids are a bore,
So that could be a plus.

He raps and he raps, so I guess 50 Cent
Is someone who'd *never* be called
Reticent.

50 *Cent* is *not* reti*cent*.

Now you:

_____

_____

_____

_____

_____

Revere

(verb) "Rih-VEER"

You **revere** someone you **respect**.
You **look up to** the guy
Without straining your neck.
If I am a person that people **revere**,
They don't think I'm pesky
Or stupid or queer.
They might even buy me a beer.

Who *didn't* revere Paul Revere?
Well, I guess the British didn't.

Now you:

_____

_____

_____

_____

_____

R

Rotund

(adj) "Roe-TUND"

A dictionary will tell you
That **rotund** means **round**.
But it kinda means **fat**.
Well, that's what I've found.

That ro*tund* guy weighs a *ton*.

Now you:

_____

_____

_____

_____

_____

Rue

(verb) "ROO"

If you **regret** a bad move,
If **you're sorry**, you **rue** it.
You simply **feel bad** and **lament**
'Cause you blew it.
If you have half a conscience,
You still **rue** the day
You forgot all your lines
And half ruined the play.

You *rue ru*ining things.

Now you:

_____

_____

_____

_____

_____

Ruminate

(verb) "ROOM-ih-nate"

It's to **contemplate a subject**;
It's to **think and think and think**.
It means **spending lots of time**
On just one thought.
If you find you're **ruminating**
On the girl your buddy's dating—
Keep your mouth shut;
Try not to get caught.

Aristotle **wondered**,
"Am I gay or am I straight?"
So he found a quiet room
Where he could sit and **ruminate**.

Your *room* is a good place to *rum*inate.

Now you:

_____

_____

_____

_____

_____

Sallow

(adj) "SAL-oe"

It simply means something all **yellow**,
Like **yellow because you look sick**.
She was **sallow** as nasty beef tallow,
And her tongue became swollen and thick.
Nice!

Alcohol causes some problems,
And one of them just makes me shiver:
You will likely turn **sallow** and **sickly**
If cirrhosis gets hold of your liver.
Ewww.
Both stanzas were nasty.

Sallow means you look sick and yallow.
Help.

Now you:

_____
_____
_____
_____
_____

Sanguine

(adj) "SANG-win"

It means you're
Hopeful, optimistic, in a mood to play.
I knew Grandma was **sanguine**
When she sang all freaking day.

Grandma *sang* when she was *sang*uine.

Now you:

_____
_____
_____
_____
_____

S

Sardonic

(adj) "Sar-DON-ik"

Smart alecky and **cynical**,
Satirical and **mean**—
These are words
That help describe **sardonic**.
Comics are **sardonic**
In their comedy routines.
Think of this: **sarcastic** meets **ironic**.

I'll tell you who's **sardonic**:
Comic writer Tina Fey.
She uses her **sarcasm** in *the funniest* way.

Sardonic=sarcastic meets ironic.

Now you:

_____

_____

_____

_____

_____

Scourge

(noun) "SKURJ"

A **scourge** is a **terrible thing or event**
That **causes widespread devastation**.
A **scourge** of great whites
In the mood for a fight
Could disfigure your surfing vacation.

Gossip could certainly be called a **scourge**
'Cause it's **negative, causing great pain**.
That's one kind of **scourge**
That you might want to purge,
Or at least show some class and refrain.

Do what you can to *scour* and *purge* a *scourge*.

Now you:

_____

_____

_____

_____

_____

Sensationalism

(noun) "Sen-SAY-shun-ul-iz-um"

It's **news** that's been put out there
Just **to feed a vulgar taste**.
It's been **designed to startle**;
Intellectually: a waste.
"Fergie Robs Convenience Store
While She's Completely Nude!"
Sensationalists print anything:
Naughty, false, or rude.

Sensationalism ain't so sensational.

Now you:

_____

_____

_____

_____

_____

Serpentine

(adj) "SER-pun-teen"

Twisting and **winding**,
You know what I mean?
Kinda **shaped like a serpent**—
That's **serpentine**.

When I hike way up high in the Malibu hills,
The **serpentine** creatures
Provide a few thrills.
You know one to see one—
There is no mistake
When you stand foot to face
With a huge rattle**snake**.

Serpentine: shaped like a serpent.

Now you:

_____

_____

_____

_____

S

Servile

(adj) "SER-vile"

Submissive and **subservient**—
Well, that's no way to be.
That would make you **servile**
And bummed, I guarantee.
Obedient can be okay.
But that's not all this means;
If you're **servile**, you're a **lap dog**.
What a way to spend your teens.

REMEMBER THIS:

*Serv*ile people *serve* other people.

Now you:

_____

_____

_____

_____

_____

Slander

(noun) "SLAN-der"

Slander is
Wicked expressions of malice,
Like throwing big, **mean verbal stones**
At the palace.

If I *say* that Tom Cruise is a weirdo,
That's **slander**;
It's libel to put it in writing.
Well, Tom Cruise *is* a weirdo,
Now, maybe he'll sue me.
Aren't **slander** and libel exciting?

REMEMBER THIS:

Slander is a verbal slam.

Now you:

_____

_____

_____

_____

_____

Solicitous

(adj) "Soe-LISS-it-us"

Attentive and **worried**
And **eager to please**.
Solicitous people
Will jump when you sneeze.
They **solicit your feelings**.
They **ask how you are**.
A **solicitous** girlfriend
Will lend you her car.

Remember that time
When a guy broke your heart?
Your friends gathered round and said,
"Make a new start!
Forget him. He's not good enough anyway."
Solicitous friends
Will know just what to say.

REMEMBER THIS:

*Solicit*ous people *solicit* your feelings.

Now you:

_____

_____

_____

_____

_____

Solvent

(adj) "SOL-vent"

This means **you have money
To pay all your debts**,
Like your Taco Bell tab
And your gambling bets.

Thanks to the way Harry Potter evolved,
The problem$ that plagued J. K. Rowling
Were $olved.

REMEMBER THIS:

If you're *solve*nt, that *solve*s your financial problems.

Now you:

_____

_____

_____

_____

_____

S

Specious

(adj) "SPEE-shus"

**Appearing to be true
But false, in fact**.
Watch out for **specious** language
In your movie contract.

On TV shows like *Gossip Girl*,
Specious leads the way
With rumors and the whispers;
People backstab and betray.

REMEMBER THIS:

Be suspicious; we're a specious species.

Now you:

_____

_____

_____

_____

_____

Spiel

(noun) "SHPEEL"

A **spiel** is an **overblown lecture**,
A **sales pitch**, or maybe a **speech**.
Blowhards are big on delivering **spiels**,
Especially on things out of reach.

Link **spiel** to that guy Steven Spielberg . . .
He makes all those big movie deals,
And I'll bet you ten bucks
That he's tired of the shmucks
Who come spouting
Their **pitches** and **spiels**.

REMEMBER THIS:

Steven *Spiel*berg hears a lot of *spiel*s.

Now you:

_____

_____

_____

_____

Staid

(adj) "STAYED"

Unemotional and **serious**
And **in control**
(or trying) . . .
That's the way you look if you are **staid**.
It's not a bad exterior to have
If you're caught lying
Or if you realize you're being played.

He was so *staid* that his expression just *stayed*.

Now you:

_____

_____

_____

_____

_____

Steadfast

(adj) "STED-fast"

Sure and **strong** . . . **reliable**.
Steadfast means you're **steady**.
You want your doctors **steadfast**:
Trusty, **true**, and **ready**.
In operating rooms,
You bet it's crucial to be **steadfast**
'Cause if a surgeon isn't . . .
Well, a patient could be dead fast.

*Stead*fast is *stead*y.

Now you:

_____

_____

_____

_____

_____

S

Stealth

(noun) "STELTH"

My cat is **sneaky** and **stealthy** and **sly**.
Believe me, it's true. Want to know why?
The other day she ran right into the house
With a green lizard's tail
Hanging out of her mouth.
She'd **sneaked** up and chomped on his tail
   (don't you doubt it),
Then the little guy ran off without it.
But that tail jumped around on my living
   room floor
For (*I am not kidding*) two minutes or more.
I know that's not really all **stealth** is about,
But I just had to tell you.
That thing freaked me out.

REMEMBER THIS:

If you're going to *steal*, be *steal*thy.

Now you:

_____

_____

_____

_____

_____

Stoic

(adj) "STOE-ik"

It's **someone who shows no evidence**
Of feeling passion or pain.
Hey, somebody hurry and help that guy.
Give him a glass of champagne
Or a knock on the head
(I mean anything).
He might think he's strong and heroic,
But if you ask me
That is no way to be,
Just standing there,
Stonefaced and **stoic**.

REMEMBER THIS:

*Sto*ic: as if made of *sto*ne.

Now you:

_____

_____

_____

_____

_____

Stolid

(adj) "STOL-id"

When your teacher
Will not change your grade . . .
When her final decision is **solid** . . .
If she just **will not budge**,
Or she just **doesn't care**,
Good luck, Pal. That teacher is **stolid**.

St*olid*=mentally thick or s*olid*.

Now you:

_____

_____

_____

_____

_____

Strident

(adj) "STRY-dent"

I think I'm due to write a dumb clue,
So here goes one for **strident**.
It's a **sound** that's **harsh** and **grating**,
And look: it rhymes with Trident.
So picture a kid at the store with his mum.
He's **screaming** for everything,
Most of all gum.
She says, "Listen, Brat,
You can stop being **strident**,
Or say a forever goodbye to the Trident!"
Yea, Mom!

He sounded way too s*trident* to deserve any
Trident.

Now you:

_____

_____

_____

_____

_____

S

Stupefied

(adj) "STOOP-ih-fide"

It means you're **stunned**,
You're **blown away**.
**So shocked you don't know
What to say**.
I met a movie star, then lied and said,
"I *wasn't* **stupefied**!"
It was that babe Orlando Bloom.
He strayed into the ladies room.
His big brown eyes were gaping wide.
Porlando, he was **stupefied**.

REMEMBER THIS:

*Stup*efied=so stunned, you're *stup*id.

Now you:

_____

_____

_____

_____

_____

Sublime

(adj) "Suh-BLIME"

Supreme or **outstanding**,
The absolute best.
The girls at the prom
Were **sublimely** dressed.

The band called **Sublime**
Chose their name very well . . .
So much better than calling the group
Really Swell.

REMEMBER THIS:

The band Sublime is sublime.

Now you:

_____

_____

_____

_____

_____

Supplant

(verb) "Suh-PLANT"

To **take the place of**. To **remove by force**.
He was **supplanted**
Because of a nasty divorce.
Supplanting can get you
A good many things;
It's the second best route
To becoming the king.
"And what might the first be?"
Do you have to ask?
Duh.
It's being *born* into the task.

REMEMBER THIS:

When you sup*plant*, you *plant* yourself in someone else's spot.

Now you:

_____

_____

_____

_____

_____

Surfeit

(noun) "SER-fit"

A **surfeit**'s a **surplus**;
It's **more than you need**.
It's simply an **excess amount**.
In my book, a **surfeit** of M&Ms
Is simply **too many** to count.

If you're cruising around
With your surf board
And discover a big hidden cove
With a **surfeit** of waves,
Stop and surf it.
It's worth every mile that you drove.

REMEMBER THIS:

If you find a cove with a *surfeit* of waves, *surf it*.

Now you:

_____

_____

_____

_____

_____

S

Surreal

(adj) "Ser-REEL"

When something **feels like it's fantasy**,
You might want to call that **surreal**,
Like a scene that appears **otherworldly**
With a **dreamy** or **vague** kind of feel.

REMEMBER THIS:

Think "sure real." . . .

If it's *surreal*, you're not *sure* if it's *real*.

Now you:

_____

_____

_____

_____

_____

Surreptitious

(adj) "Ser-up-TISH-us"

It's **sneaky** and **stealthy** . . .
It's **done on the sly**.
Jason Biggs **surreptitiously**
Loved apple pie.

When I was in college, we'd go to IHOP
(Just give me a minute to brag) . . .
I was **covert** and **crafty**
And so **surreptitious**
To stuff *syrup* packs in my bag.
Plus extra salt shakers, the sugar, the jam,
And those mini containers of honey . . .
Look,
When you run your own budget at school,
You have to save up for beer money.

REMEMBER THIS:

I *surrep*titiously stashed the *syrup* from IHOP.

Now you:

_____

_____

_____

_____

_____

Sycophant

(noun) "SIK-uh-fant"

Sycophants will make you sick
As **they kiss up**
And **suck up**
(Again, I may chuck up).

They'll **flatter** and **follow you all around**.
They'll pick up whatever
You drop on the ground.
Don't keep **sycophants**
In your close entourage.
They **act like they're friends**,
But it's just a mirage.

REMEMBER THIS:

Sycophants make me sick.

Now you:

_____

_____

_____

_____

_____

Tautology

(noun) "Taw-TOL-uh-jee"

Tautology is **repetition**,
You **communicate but without thrift**.
You say what is clearly **repetitive**:
Like *tall giant* or here's a *free gift*.

When your sentences sound **tautological**,
You're writing without enough thought.
I will bet that this mindless expression
Is not what your teachers have taught.

REMEMBER THIS:

You weren't *taught* to repeat yourself with *taut*ology.

(Hey, that statement was tautologous.)

Now you:

_____

_____

_____

_____

_____

T

Temerity

(noun) "Teh-MARE-ih-tee"

Temerity is **brashness, recklessness,**
And **risk**.
You might not look both ways—
You jump right in.
Given that King Hank the Eighth
Would whack off women's heads,
The **temerity** crown goes to Anne Boleyn.

I'll bet you he said,
"Have you lost your fool head?
You must have a ton of **temerity**.
Haven't you heard
Of the way I treat wives?
You sure are a brave one to marry me."

REMEMBER THIS:

Remember King Henry's Words:
"She had the temerity to marry me."

Now you:

_____
_____
_____
_____
_____

Tempestuous

(adj) "Tem-PEST-yoo-us"

You've read some Bill Shakespeare,
Now haven't you?
The Tempest should help you today.
The first act begins
With a butt-kicking storm—
A **tempestuous** one, you might say.

Violent, stormy, and **turbulent**.
That's what **tempestuous** means.
I once threw a bash so **tempestuous**
The neighbors called in the Marines.

REMEMBER THIS:

Shakespeare's *The Tempest* begins with a
*tempest*uous storm.
*Or Temp*estuous teens lose their *temp*ers.

Now you:

_____
_____
_____
_____
_____

Tenacious

(adj) "Ten-AY-shus"

Time for another stupid clue.
Tenacious is the word we'll do.
It means **persistent, won't give in**.
Tenacious athletes tend to win.

So think: **tenacious** tennis player . . .
In over his head, he hasn't a prayer,
But thanks to **persistence**
He'll never forget,
He smashes *ten aces* to win the last set.

The *tenacious* tennis player served *ten aces*.

Now you:

_____

_____

_____

_____

_____

Timorous

(adj) "TIM-er-us"

It's **timid** and **anxious**.
It means **full of fear**.
A **timorous** creature's a rabbit or deer.

You read of that poor little guy Tiny Tim?
Dickens described him as **timorous**, grim.
Lucky for him, Mr. Scrooge took him in
And served Reese's Pieces
To make him less thin.
Or not.

*Tim*orous means *tim*id, like Tiny *Tim*.

Now you:

_____

_____

_____

_____

_____

T

Toady

(noun) "TOE-dee"

What a great word.
Is it silly enough?
It means you're a **flattering suck up**.
Just like the **obsequious** girl I described,
A **toady** makes me want to chuck up.
You know all those chicks
Who **suck up** to rock stars?
They are the worst kind of **toadies**.
In order to get with the headlining band,
They pretend that they like
The band's roadies.

Toadies suck up to bands' roadies.

Now you:

_____

_____

_____

_____

_____

Tome

(noun) "TOME"

A **really long book—big and heavy**.
If you have a **tome** that you hate,
Don't bother complaining about it;
A **tome** is a great paperweight.

War and Peace is by old Leo Tolstoy,
And all around Russia it roams.
That thing's over twelve hundred pages!
It's one of the classic old **tomes**.

It takes a lot of time to read a tome.

Now you:

_____

_____

_____

_____

_____

Tractable

(adj) "TRAKT-uh-bul"

If you're **easy to manage**,
Then we call you **tractable**.
Your opinions and actions
Are very **impactable**.
You might **acquiesce**,
And you might be **servile** . . .
I don't know about you,
But that sure ain't *my* style.
Being told what to do is completely uncool,
So my mother says
I'm **tractable** as a mule.

It's easy to keep *trac*table people on *track*.

Now you:

_____

_____

_____

_____

_____

Transient

(adj) "TRANZ-ee-ent"

It's **short lived** and **fleeting**
(Like good business meetings);
It's **staying a very short while**.
My sister is one very **transient** girl;
Pack up and go—that's her style.
Always **in transit**:
She's **here and then gone**.
She'll drop in, then quickly announce:
"It's been good to see ya . . .
I'm off to Korea.
I'll miss ya, but I gotta bounce."

A *trans*ient person is often in *trans*it.

Now you:

_____

_____

_____

_____

_____

T

Truculent

(adj) "TRUK-yoo-lent"

Hostile and **brutal**, **belligerent**, **cruel**
Is a **truculent** verbal attack.
A **truculent** toast or celebrity roast
Feels like one big emotional smack.

You know of those sites:
TMZ, Perez Hilton?
Some people think that they suck
'Cause they're **spiteful** and **biting**
(Yet somehow inviting);
The actors feel hit by a truck.

REMEMBER THIS:

*Truc*ulence is like being hit by a *truck*.

Now you:

_____

_____

_____

_____

_____

Truncated

(adj) "TRUN-kay-ted"

When something has been **shortened**
Or been **chopped**, it's been **truncated**.
Like a book **hacked** into SparkNotes
(That shortcut's overrated).

Think of **chopping down** a tree—
It's now become a trunk,
So the tree has been **truncated**;
(I'll bet it's in a funk).

REMEMBER THIS:

A tree *trunk* is a *trunc*ated tree.

Now you:

_____

_____

_____

_____

_____

Ubiquitous

(adj) "Yoo-BIK-wit-us"

It's **something that seems**
To exist everywhere,
Like a spooky, **ubiquitous** fog.
We'd better knock off this polluting,
My friends,
Or we'll choke on **ubiquitous** smog.

Ubiquitous entities are **all around**.
It seems that they simply **won't quit**.
Those **ubiquitous**
Trash-spreading magazines
Truly make me want to spit.

REMEMBER THIS:

Notice "quit" in the word . . .
Something ubi*quit*ous won't *quit*.

Now you:

_____

_____

_____

_____

_____

Unkempt

(adj) "Un-KEMPT"

Let me attempt to describe **unkempt**:
It's **sloppy**, **disheveled**, and **rough**.
Unkempt can be **slimy**
And **vulgar** and **skuzzy** . . .
Alright, alright . . . enough.

What the heck, I'll reference Shrek:
He's an **unkempt**, adorable dope.
Now that he's married,
You'd think he would bathe,
But he's probably eating the soap.

REMEMBER THIS:

*Unk*empt is *unc*lean.

Now you:

_____

_____

_____

_____

_____

U

Urbane

(adj) "Er-BANE"

Urbane is **sophisticated**, **elegant**, **cool**.
Who's the most **urbane** kid in your school?
An **urbane** guy has **manners**
As a general rule.
He holds the door open for girls
(He's no fool).

REMEMBER THIS:

Urbane=Elegant, like champagne.

Now you:

_____

_____

_____

_____

_____

Vacillate

(verb) "VASS-ih-late"

It's really **indecisive**,
With choices **back and forth**.
A **vacillating** tour guide
Might lead you south _and_ north.

I know a tennis player
Whose serve is freaking great,
But he loses lots of matches
Because he **vacillates**.

REMEMBER THIS:

If you vaci_llate_ you might be _late_.

Now you:

_____

_____

_____

_____

_____

Vacuous

(adj) "VAK-yoo-us"

Without any content,
Like **stupid**, **inane**.
Do you know anyone
With a **vacuous** brain?
How 'bout Paris Hilton?
She's **empty** and cheesy.
Yeah, I bashed her again . . .
She just makes it so easy.

REMEMBER THIS:

She's as *vacu*ous as a new *vacu*um bag.

Now you:

_____

_____

_____

_____

_____

Vapid

(adj) "VA-pid"

Lifeless, **insipid,** and **generally flat**.
Vapid is **boring**.
How thrilling is that?
My brother's prom date
Was as **vapid** as vapor.
He spent the whole night
Wishing he could escape her.

REMEMBER THIS:

*Vap*id=Lifeless as *vap*or.

Now you:

_____

_____

_____

_____

_____

Verbose
(adj) "Ver-BOSE"

Verbose teachers **use too many words**.
They **talk** and they **talk**
'Til your hearing is blurred.
A **verbose** person can bore you to death.
Shut up, already!
We're all out of breath.

*Verb*ose people use too many *verb*s.

Now you:

_____

_____

_____

_____

_____

Veritable
(adj) "VARE-ih-tuh-bul"

It means **authentic**, **sure**, and **real**
With **nothing sneaky to conceal**.
Remember: "***Very little bull.***"
Now there's a concept that's ideal.

I'm glad that Justin Timberlake
Did not turn out to be a fake.
He started with an all-boy band,
And frankly those are hard to take.
Sometimes they're no more than cute,
But Justin has the skills to boot.
He's **veritable**, artist-wise,
So give him a salute.

If it's *veritable*, there's *verylittlebull*.

Now you:

_____

_____

_____

_____

_____

Vilify

(verb) "VIL-uh-fy"

To **speak badly of**, to **slander, defame**.
To **make one the villain**.
To **give him the blame**.
Like in old Western movies,
There's always that stranger they all **vilify**,
And he's in big danger.

As the men of the town
Ride in search of a **villain**,
They whoop "Giddyup yo!
There's gonna be killin'!"
When it comes to a stranger,
They can't help temptation
To saddle on up for some **vilification**.

REMEMBER THIS:

To *vili*fy is to make a *vill*ain out of someone.

Now you:

_____

_____

_____

_____

_____

Virtuoso

(noun) "Ver-choo-OE-so"

Virtuosos—
They are **talented** . . .
And **well above the rest**.
In science, sports, or music
Virtuosos are the best.
A classic **virtuoso**
Is the famous Tiger Woods.
He's a **virtuoso**
'Cause he's **oh so good**.

REMEMBER THIS:

A virtu*oso* is *oh so* good.

Now you:

_____

_____

_____

_____

_____

Volition

(noun) "Voe-LISH-un"

Volition is **power to do as you please**,
No help from outside,
No down on your knees.
If you want something badly,
Remember **volition**;
It's **all up to you**,
So don't waste your time wishin'.
Think of it this way:
It's all **voluntary**.
Someday you might use **volition** to marry,
That is, if the marriage thing isn't too scary.

Your *voli*tion is *vol*untary.

Now you:

_____

_____

_____

_____

_____

Voluble

(adj) "VOL-yuh-bul"

This one means **yakky** and **talkative**;
It's **garrulous** and it's **verbose**.
I'm thinking of **voluble** daytime TV.
Let's face it: most talk shows are gross.

The word means
You're **speaking in volumes**,
And most people think that it's bad.
Tell a **voluble** teacher,
"Hey, wrap it up, Pal!"
And you'll make
The whole lecture hall glad.

*Volu*ble people speak *volu*mes.

Now you:

_____

_____

_____

_____

_____

Wheedle

(verb) "WEE-dul"

Remember I said that you ought to **cajole**
In a theater group
When you want the lead role?
Well, **wheedle**—
That word means essentially the same.
It's really **cajole** with a weasely name.

If you **persuade** or **influence**
By flattering,
If you **brownnose** and **B.S.**,
If you **do what you have to**
To get what you want,
You're a **wheedling** weasel, I guess.

REMEMBER THIS:

If you always wheedle, you're kind of a weasel.

Now you:

_____

_____

_____

_____

_____

Winsome

(adj) "WIN-sum"

It's **charming** or **engaging**,
Often **in a childlike way**.
A **winsome** smile says,
"Bring it on. I'm gladly led astray."

Patrick Dempsey has a **winsome** smile,
And so does Halle Berry.
Their kids would be **winsome**thing-else;
Maybe they should marry.

REMEMBER THIS:

You'll _win some_ people with a _winsome_ smile.

Now you:

_____

_____

_____

_____

_____

Wizened

(adj) "WIZ-und"

Wizenend means
Withered and **shriveled**.
It means that you're **looking quite old**.
Before you'll be wise,
Must you have **wizened** eyes?
If that's how it works, Man that's cold.

REMEMBER THIS:

The old *wiz*ard was *wiz*ened.

Now you:

_____

_____

_____

_____

_____

Zealous

(adj) "ZELL-us"

Zealous means **enthused**,
It means you're **psyched**,
You're **fired up**!
Get **zealous** about the SAT,
And maybe your score won't suck.

REMEMBER THIS:

Zealous **DOES NOT** mean jealous!!!!
See how fired up *I sound*?

Now you:

_____

_____

_____

_____

_____

Zenith

(noun) "ZEE-nith"

The **zenith** is the **high point**,
The **highest you can reach**.
The **zenith** of my whole career
Is having you brats to teach.
Good one.

REMEMBER THIS:

When a star is at its zenith, you can barely
seenith.

Wow, that was bad.

Now you:

_____

_____

_____

_____

_____

Z

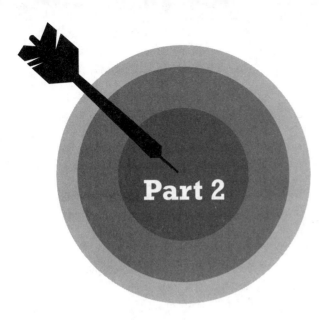

Part 2

The Roots

Know some Greek and Latin
If you want to be smart.
This is just a sample,
But at least it's a start.

Roots will help you figure out what many words mean.
Stay awake, and you'll become a verbal machine.
Again, you'll find the many definitions **in bold**.
Damn, this book is fun to read,
Or so I've been told.

AC, ACR
Sharp, Sour

Acrid
("AK-rid")

Acrimonious
("AK-rih-MONE-ee-us")

Acerbic
("Uh-SER-bik")

Acuity
("Uh-KYOO-ih-tee")

Acute
("Uh-KYOOT")

An **acrid** taste is sour.
Acrid comments **tend to bite**.
Her daughter's **acrid** tendencies
Are wicked **impolite**.

When someone's **acrimonious**,
Just leave the guy alone.
He's **caustic** and he's **bitter**—
Doesn't have a funny bone.

Acerbic is the same
Because it's **sharp** and **harsh** and **sour**.
Acerbic people always seem to
Bad-mouth and devour.

Acuity is different;
It's a **sharpness**, but it's **good**.
If you're verbally **acute**,
Your words are often understood.

Now you:

_____

_____

_____

_____

_____

BEL, BELL
War

Bellicose
("BELL-ih-kose")

Rebellion
("Ree-BELL-yun")

Belligerent
("Bell-IJ-er-ent")

Antebellum
("AN-tee-BELL-um")

If you're **eager to fight**, you are called **bellicose**.
Do me a favor, and don't get too close.
I've already spoken about a **rebellion**:
An **uprising** that could begin with a hellion.

A **belligerent** kid's kinda **hostile** and **scrappy**,
Not one to make babysitters too happy.
And here's what those great dictionaries are for:
Look up **antebellum**. It's *before* **the war**.

Now you:

_____

_____

_____

_____

_____

CHRON
Time

Chronological
("Kron-ih-LOJ-ih-kul")

Synchronized
("SINK-ruh-nized")

Chronicle
("KRON-ih-kul")

Anachronous
("An-AK-ruh-nus")

This one should be easy. It's all about **time**,
So let's move through it quickly
With short, little rhymes.
Chronological means **in order of time**.
Synchronized: **at the same rate**.
My sister tried **synchronized** swimming with me;
We looked like two squid on a plate.

A **chronicle** narrates **historic events**.
Anachronous: **in the *wrong* time**.
To show a laptop in a Civil War film
Would be an **anachronous** crime.

Now you:

____

____

____

____

____

CLAUS, CLOIS, CLUD, CLUS
Close, Shut

Recluse
("REK-loos")

Cloister
("KLOY-ster")

Preclude
("Pree-KLOOD")

Occlude
("Uh-KLOOD")

You know **claustrophobia, include** and **exclude**—
Let's do some more.
Yahoo. Yipee, Dude.
A **recluse** is **someone who doesn't go out**.
A **reclusive** guy makes a lame Eagle Scout.

A **cloister's secluded**, a nice **private place**.
That sounds like a very cool songwriting space.
Preclude is **eliminate, get in the way**—
Weak ankles **precluded** her life of ballet.

To **block** or **obstruct**:
That means to **occlude**.
Country clubs might **occlude** anyone who's tattooed
Or verbally crude
Or frequently nude . . .
How stuffy and rude!

Now you:

_____

_____

_____

_____

_____

CULP
Blame, Fault

Culpable
("KUL-puh-bul")

Exculpated
("EX-kul-pay-ted")

Culprit
("KUL-prit")

Mea Culpa
("MAY-uh KUL-puh")

It has to do with **blame** or **fault**;
"I'm **culpable** for the assault."

If you've been **exculpated**,
They **let you off the hook.**
You got away, you **culprit**
(Which means a slippery **crook**).

Mea culpa. Look! More Latin!
It's "**I did it**" or "**My bad**."
Just say **mea culpa**,
And you'll make the judge less mad.

Now you:

_____

_____

_____

_____

_____

DICT
Say, Tell, Word

Jurisdiction
("Jer-iss-DIK-shun")

Benediction
("Ben-ih-DIK-shun")

Indict
("In-DITE")

You know **dictionary**, **verdict**, and **predict**
Without a blink;
I'll bet you know a lot more of this root than you think.

Jurisdiction . . . **Jurisdiction** . . . see it this way:
It means **within a range**
Where certain *juries* have a *say*.
So if you break the law
And you're within my **jurisdiction**
(That is if I'm a judge),
I might just hand you a conviction.

Benediction is **a blessing**
That's bestowed on your head—
Words of good will, if you're alive or you're dead.
If you're chosen as the one to give the **benediction**,
Try hard not to laugh. Stand up and say it with conviction.
Now check out **indict**
(Why does it rhyme with "invite"?):
It means that you're **officially accused**.
On the day he was **indicted**,
Al Capone appeared excited,
And the jury pool was thoroughly confused.

Now you:

_____

_____

_____

_____

_____

EU
Good, Well

Eurhythmic
("Yoo-RITH-mik")

Euphoric
("Yoo-FOR-ik")

Euthanasia
("YOO-thuh-NAY-zhuh")

Eugenics
("Yoo-JEN-iks")

Eurythmical sounds are quite **pleasing**.
They're in a **harmonious order**.
If you hear Annie Lennox beginning to sing,
Grab a good mic and record her.

And if you are feeling **euphoric**,
You're **happy** and **floating on clouds**.
Most people don't feel too **euphoric**
In traffic or crammed into crowds.

And let's not forget **euthanasia** . . .
It's also known as **mercy killing**.
It's to **painlessly put a sick person to death**.
That is, if the person is willing.

Eugenics:
The study of **breeding**
A much more desirable race.
It's **choosing which genes should go forward**.
I'll take Kate Beckinsale's face.

Now you:

_____

_____

_____

_____

_____

FIN
End, Limit

Finale
("Fin-AL-ee")

Refine
("Ree-FINE")

Ad Infinitum
("Ad In-fih-NITE-um")

Definitive
("Deh-FIN-ih-tiv")

Final and **finally, finalize, infinite,**
Finish and **finite** and **finalist** . . .
These are just some of the words based on **FIN**
That belong on your "Duh, Yeah, I Know" list.

But there's also **finale** (it rhymes with "the valley");
It's the **ending routine of a show**.
And then there's **refine** (as in sugar or wine);
It's to **purify** (like driven snow).

And let me suggest, if you know of a guest
Who plans to stay **ad infinitum** . . .
That means that the guy's **never leaving** your house,
So here's just a thought: don't invite him.

A **definitive** work: **the best source you can get**.
It's **reliable** as it can be.
This is, in fact, the **definitive** work
For learning vocabulary.
(*Woohoo! Way to go, me!*)

Now you:

_____

_____

_____

_____

_____

GEN
Birth, Origin, Race, Type

Genetics
("Jen-ET-iks")

Genealogy
("Jeen-ee-OL-uh-jee")

Generate
("JEN-er-ate")

Pathogen
("PATH-uh-jen")

Genetics is the **science of heredity**;
It **studies inherited genes**.
Genetics can help you interpret
Why your hair is all kinky and green
And why you're built like a Marine.

If you study your own **genealogy**,
Then you're into your **family history**.
Hey, dig up that story of Grandpa
That everyone calls "The Big Mystery."

If you **generate** lots of excitement,
If your friends say you **generate** fun,
You **produce** it or **give it existence**.
Then you're wanted by everyone.

A **pathogen causes diseases**;
It could be a **virus** or **fungus**,
So go wash your hands just as much as you can
Because **pathogens** travel among us.

Now you:

_____

_____

_____

_____

_____

GNOR, GNOS
Know

Cognizant
("KOG-nih-zunt")

Incognito
("In-kog-NEE-toe")

Prognosis
("Prog-NOE-sis")

Agnostic
("Ag-NOS-tik")

Ignorant and **recognize** . . .
You already know of those two guys,
So here are more of gnos and gnor;
To help you join the wise . . .

Cognizant means **having awareness of**:
I'm **cognizant** of my mother's love.
To be **incognito**, **disguise** who you are.
Wear dark glasses indoors,
Like a big movie star.

A doctor's **prognosis** is just a **prediction**
Of **how you'll come out** of your latest affliction.
Agnostics will **question, express lots of doubt**.
They're **not sure there's a God**.
"What's this church thing about?"

Now you:

_____

_____

_____

_____

_____

GRAD, GRESS
Step

Gradient
("GRAY-dee-ent")

Transgression
("Tranz-GRESH-in")

Ingress
("IN-gress")

Egress
("EE-gress")

Plenty from this root group are familiar, I guess,
Like **graduate** and **gradual**, like **grades** and
   progress.

The **gradient** of something is **degree of inclination**.
Colorado's **gradients** are great for ski vacations.
I'm a total baby when it comes to downhill speed;
Bunny hills have all the thrills and **gradients** I need.

Committing a **transgression** is like **making a mistake**.
To **overstep**, to **violate**—to **sin**, for God's sake!
The Ambassador to England made a royal impression
When he pinched the queen's bum.
You might call that a **transgression**.

Ingress means **going in**, egress means **going out**.
They're nouns that seem like verbs.
Huh? What is *that* all about?
There was a huge **ingress**
(Or you might also say **ingression**)
Into the studio to hear The Beatles's last jam session.
Bobby's nervous parents stopped their son from **egress**.
They didn't want him prancing round the yard in a dress.

Now you:

_____

_____

_____

_____

_____

JUR
Law, Swear

Perjure
("PER-jer")

Jurisprudence
("Jer-iss-PROO-dents")

Conjure
("KON-jer")

Adjure
("Uh-JER")

Abjure
("Ab-JER")

If you **perjure** yourself, you will likely regret it.
It's to **lie under oath** . . .
Ooooooh . . . *you're gonna getttt it.*
(Sing that last part.)

The **philosophy of law** is called **jurisprudence**—
Not too exciting, unless you're law students.
To **conjure**: **produce** or **bring into existence**.
She **conjured** a yacht with the wizard's assistance.

"**Please** tell the truth
And make sure that you're sure . . ."
If I ask you this way, you could say I **adjure**.
Adjuring is **solemnly asking**, **entreating** . . .
The teacher **adjured** him to knock off the cheating.
Abjuring is **giving up**, **shunning**, **renouncing**.
She **abjured** all the drugs
And then left the room bouncing.

Now you:

_____

_____

_____

_____

_____

LUC, LUM
Light

Pellucid
("Peh-LOO-sid")

Elucidate
("Ee-LOO-sih-date")

Illuminate
("Ih-LOO-mih-nate")

Luminary
("LOO-mih-nare-ee")

Lucid
("LOO-sid")

Pellucid means **transparent**.
It's **translucent** and it's **clear**.
I try to write **pellucidly**;
It's big in my career.

Give us **clear descriptions**, and you're an **elucidator**.
If you like **elucidating**
Why not be an educator?

To **illuminate** a subject
Makes it clear (like a good writer).
Illuminate the room, and now the place
Is that much **brighter**.
A **luminary gives off light**,
Like when a rocket's firing.
It can also mean **celebrity**,
Someone you find inspiring.

Lucid can mean **simply understood** or **clear** or **sane**.
Grandma's ninety-eight and **lucid**;
That old gal should not complain.

Now you:

_____

_____

_____

_____

_____

MAGN
Great, Large

Magnanimous
("Mag-NAN-ih-mus")

Magnum
("MAG-num")

Magnum Opus
("MAG-num OE-pus")

Magnitude
("MAG-nih-tood")

Magnate
("MAG-nate")

Magniloquent
("Mag-NIL-uh-kwent")

A **magnanimous** person has a **really big heart**.
His **kindness** and **forgiveness** are what set him apart.
(Show that you're **magnanimous**
And buy me pricey art.)

A **magnum** bottle holds **a lot** of champagne or wine.
A **magnum opus** is a **work of art** that's divine.
(It's probably that **artist's best** success of all time.)
For Oprah's **magnum opus**
She might donate every dime.

The **magnitude** of something is its **greatness of size**,
And **magnates own big companies**
(You've heard of these guys . . .
They might be rich, they might be wise . . .
Or simply weasels in disguise).

Magniloquent speech is kind of **pompous** and **loud**.
Fathead politicians talk this way to a crowd.

Now you:

_____

_____

_____

_____

MAL
Bad

This is a big one, so let's get it straight.
This prefix is all about **badness** and **hate**.

Malicious
("Muh-LISH-iss")

A guy who's **malicious** is really quite **vicious**;
He **causes great pain** with great ease.
And get this: **malicious** is also **pernicious**
(Which you read all about in the Ps).

Malevolent
("Muh-LEV-uh-lent")

Malevolent people are kind of the same
As the guy I just spoke of above.
They're all about **darkness** and **damage** and **evil**.
You will not be feeling the love.

Malfeasance
("Mal-FEEZ-ense")

Malediction
("Mal-ih-DIK-shun")

Malfeasance is another way to say **crime**.
Be a **malfeasant**, and you'll do the time.
And avoid **malediction**: a **hex** or a **curse**.
Enrage an old witch, and you might ride the hearse.

Malaise
("Muh-LAZE")

Malady
("MAL-uh-dee")

If you're feeling **malaise**, you are **weak** or **diseased**,
Or maybe it's just that you feel **ill at ease**.
A **malady**'s kind of the same as **malaise**.
So many synonyms . . .
I'm in a daze.

Now you:

_____

_____

_____

_____

_____

MIS
Bad, **Hate**, **Wrong**

Misogynist
("Mih-SOJ-in-ist")

Misapprehend
("Mis-ap-ree-HEND")

Misanthrope
("MIS-in-thrope")

Mishap
("MIS-hap")

Misunderstand, mistake, mistrust . . .
This list could go on and on, so
Knowing this prefix is surely a must.

A **person who hates women** is a **misogynist**.
He probably hated his mother,
And I'll bet you he ain't getting kissed.

To **misapprehend** is to **misunderstand**.
If you **misapprehend** as you read
The directions on cough syrup bottles,
You might chug a lot more than you need.

And if you should find that you **hate humankind**,
Then you're just a big **misanthrope**.
If you had your way, we would all hang and sway
From a very long, thick piece of rope.

A **mishap** is **bad luck**, an **accident**.
It's a **screw up** you'd like to reverse,
Like that time that you ate too much crap at the fair
And barfed in your aunt's Gucci purse.

Now you:

_____

_____

_____

_____

_____

NEC, NECR
Death

Necropolis
("Neh-KROP-uh-liss")

Necromancy
("NEK-ruh-man-see")

Necrosis
("Neh-KROE-siss")

Necrophile
("NEK-ruh-file")

Couldn't help dragging in this one.
Too creepy and dark to resist.
Let's start the list off with **necropolis**.
It's the **place where dead people exist**.

Necromancy is like witchcraft,
When you **speak to those already dead**.
A **necrology**'s like an **obituary**.
How many of those have you read?

Necrosis means **death of the body**,
As in some of the **tissues or cells**.
It could happen from trauma or illness.
Either way, the thing probably smells.

If audiophiles know about stereos,
And bibliophiles love lots of books,
Necrophiles are **into dead people**.
They must get their share of weird looks.

Now you:

_____

_____

_____

_____

_____

NOM, NYM | 191

NOM, NYM
Name

You know **synonym** and **anonymous** too . . .
Here's a little more of that root thing you do . . .

Nomenclature
("NOE-men-klay-cher")

Misnomer
("Mis-NOE-mer")

Pseudonym
("SOO-doe-nim")

Ignominious
("Ig-noe-MIN-ee-us")

**Nomenclature: terms that guide
An industry or group**.
Learn the **nomenclature**, and you're good;
You'll know the scoop

A **misnomer** is when **something
Has been given the wrong name**,
Like naming your dog Killer
Though he's wimpy and tame.

You want **to write in secret**?
Then create a **pseudonym**.
Mark Twain was Samuel Clemens;
Please say you've heard of him!

Ignominious moments
Cause you shame, humiliation.
They hurt your family **name**.
They give no cause for celebration
(Don't trip and fall at graduation).

Now you:

_____

_____

_____

_____

_____

OMNI
All

Omnivorous
("Om-NIV-er-us")

Omniscient
("Om-NIH-shint")

Omnipotent
("Om-NIH-puh-tent")

Omni is one that you're sure to recall—
It means **everything**,
As in **totally, all**.

Omnivorous eaters will **eat anything**.
Omniscient investors end up with the bling
Because they **know all** about stock marketing.

Omnipotent people **have all of the power**;
They conquer and trample and rule and devour.

Now you:

_____

_____

_____

_____

PAN
All

Panacea
("Pan-uh-SEE-uh")

Panegyric
("Pan-ih-JEER-ik")

Panoply
("PAN-uh-plee")

Pandemic
("Pan-DEM-ik")

A **cure-all** is a **panacea**.
It **fixes the whole wretched mess**.
Gambling is no **panacea**
To **cure** your financial distress.

A **panegyric expresses approval**.
It's a **speech** or **adoring oration**.
I'll happily write one about you
In exchange for a modest donation.

Panoply—this word is easy;
It's a **vast** and **impressive display**.
I stared at the massive Grand Canyon;
Its **panoply** blew me away.

And **pandemic** means **universal**
Or **spreading all over the place**.
Pandemic world hunger is awful.
It's truly a **global** disgrace.

Now you:

_____

_____

_____

_____

_____

PARA
Beside, Resembling

Parable
("PARE-uh-bul")

Paranoia
("PARE-uh-NOY-uh")

Paramedic
("PARE-uh-MED-ik")

Paralegal
("PARE-uh-LEE-gul")

Paradigm
("PARE-uh-dime")

Paradox
("PARE-uh-dox")

A **parable** is a **short story**
Designed to teach us a moral.
The lesson's **beside** the story,
Which might be written, might be oral.

Paranoia brings **suspicion**, **nervousness**, and **doubt**.
You think nobody's truthful—
Even Bambi freaks you out.

Paramedics can help like physicians.
They're great if no doctor's around.
Paralegals are helpful to lawyers,
And they're often much less tightly wound.

A **paradigm** serves as a **model**.
It's the **pattern** you might want to **follow**.
A **paradigm** can **guide** your project,
So you don't sit around and just wallow.

A **paradox** is a **statement**
Or situation that contradicts.
Sometimes it's a **dilemma**
That you **can't figure out** how to fix.

Now you:

_____

_____

_____

_____

_____

PATH, PATHY
Feeling, Illness, Suffering

Sympathy
("SIM-puh-thee")

Empathy
("EM-puh-thee")

Antipathy
("An-TIH-puh-thee")

Pathos
("PAY-those")

Pathology
("Puh-THOL-uh-jee")

Telepathy
("Tel-EP-uh-thee")

Sympathy and **empathy**? They're related, in a sense,
But here's an explanation that will show the difference:
You feel **sympathy**
Because of what **your friend is going through**,
But with **empathy it's like it's happening to you**.
Sympathy will say, "**I'm sorry. I feel bad** for you."
Empathy will say, "**I'm sorry. I have been there**, too."

Anti means **against**. But you kind of knew that, right?
Antipathy is **hatred**, a **habitual dislike**.
I tend to have **antipathy** toward ugly, racist jokes.
You know of my **antipathy** for cigarettes and smoke.

Pathos causes feelings—as in **pity**, **pain**, or **strife**.
It's found in art, like songs
That **make you ache** about your life
(Just don't go reaching for a knife).

Pathology's the **study of the nature of disease**.
A **pathologist** does **research**; it's a needed expertise.

Telepathy sends messages between two brains.
During finals, why not spy on what your teacher's head
    contains?

Now you:

_____

_____

_____

_____

_____

PEN, PUN
Punish, **Regret**

Penitentiary
("Pen-ih-TEN-shuh-ree")

Penance
("PEN-ense")

Penitent
("PEN-ih-tent")

Repent
("Ree-PENT")

Impunity
("Im-PYOON-ih-tee")

Punitive
("PYOON-ih-tiv")

Penology
("Pen-OL-uh-jee")

So you know about **penitentiaries**—
Those are just **prisons** or **jails**.
Some were created for women,
But most of them house creepy males.

Penance you **pay** when you've been a **bad** boy.
Penitent people **do not jump for joy**
'Cause they **feel really sorry** for what they destroy.

"**Repent**!" Preachers shout to those who commit sin.
They want all the sinners to **feel the chagrin**.
They basically want you to turn yourself in.

If you've been **exempted** or granted **impunity**,
Goody, **you're safe**; it's just like an **immunity**.

Punitive parents won't give you the car.
They **punish** their kids; they might take your guitar.
(*You shouldn't have stolen that cash from the jar.*)

The word that means **study of prisons or crime**
Is **penology**; it's **learning about doing time**.

Now you:

_____

_____

_____

_____

_____

PRO
Ahead, Forth

Proclivity
("Proe-KLIV-ih-tee")

Profuse
("Proe-FYOOS")

Progeny
("PROJ-ih-nee")

Promontory
("PROM-in-tor-ee")

You can see **move ahead**
In these words that you know:
There's **propel** and **provoke** and **proceed**.
And you know how I love to annoy you,
So here are a few more you need:

A **proclivity** for something is a **natural inclination**.
I have a big **proclivity** for ritzy, French vacations.

If you donate things **profusely**,
You are **generous** and **giving**.
You simply give **in great amounts**.
That sounds like healthy living.

Progenies are **offspring**, **descendents** from a line.
The Jolie-Pitts are **progenies**
Whose lips should be divine.

Promontories are
High bluffs projecting toward the sea.
Careful . . .
Don't lean too far out, or you'll be beach debris.

Now you:

_____

_____

_____

_____

_____

PUG, PUGN
Fight, Fist

Pugilist
("PYOO-jil-ist")

Pugnacious
("Pug-NAY-shus")

Impugn
("Im-PYOON")

A **pugilist** is a **fighter**, someone into **war**.
Remind me,
What is it we need this kind of person for?
So maybe it's a **boxer**—he's a guy who fights as work.
Or a **pugilist** might simply be a dumb, **aggressive**
 jerk.

Pugnacious people **like to fight**.
They **punch** and **slap** and **kick** and **bite**.
If you hang out with someone **pugnacious**,
Make sure that the room is spacious.

To **impugn** is to **cast doubt upon**,
To **challenge** or **attack**.
If I **impugn** yo mama,
You might give me a smack.

What about those pug dogs?
Are they little pugly **fighters**?
I guess it's not their fault
They look like ugly, pugly biters.

Now you:

_____

_____

_____

_____

_____

SACR, SANC, SECR
Sacred

Sacrosanct
("SAK-roe-sankt")

Sanction
("SANK-shun")

Consecrate
("KON-seh-krate")

Desecrate
("DES-eh-krate")

Sanctity
("SANK-tih-tee")

Sacrosanct means **sacred, should not be changed**.
When someone's house is **sacrosanct**, it feels
a little strange.
My publishers believe my vocab book is **sacrosanct**.
Trust me, in Christmas cards this year they'll be thanked.

Sanction is **approval**. You might **sanction** a law.
If you don't **sanction** a war, you want to withdraw.

Something **consecrated** has been **blessed** or
set apart.
It's labeled **special, sacred, near to somebody's
heart**.
But **desecrated**—that's another story, oh boy.
It's to **violate the sacredness**, **defile**, or **destroy**.
If you **desecrate** a church, you're gonna break
a few hearts.
If you **desecrate** your school, well, Champ, that ain't
very smart.

The **sanctity** of something is its **state of being holy**.
The **sanctity** of marriage? Trust me: enter it slowly.

Now you:

_____

_____

_____

_____

_____

SCI, SCIEN
Know

Conscience
("KON-shense")

Conscientious
("KON-shee-EN-shus")

Prescient
("PRESH-ent")

Omniscient
("Om-NIH-shent")

It's "scien," as in **knowledge**.
That's why **scientists** go to college.

If you have a **conscience**,
You can tell wrong from right.
Show you have a **conscience**—
Get your butt home tonight.

When you're **conscientious** you are **careful** and **just**.
Conscientious babysitters earn a lot of trust.

Prescient people **tell the future**. Isn't that great?
They can tell you **what will happen**
On your next blind date.

Omniscient is **all-knowing**.
To me, that skill is major.
I'm sure that you're **omniscient**
Just because you're a teenager.

Now you:

_____

_____

_____

_____

_____

SCRIPT
Write

To **script** something is to **write** it,
And a **film's written form** is a script.
Without such a thing as this **screenplay**,
A director would be unequipped.

Conscription
("Kun-SKRIP-shun")

Inscription
("In-SKRIP-shun")

If you undergo a **conscription**,
You've been **registered for war**.
You might end up being a **soldier**
'Cause that's what the **draft** is for.

Transcribe
("Tran-SKRIBE")

An **inscription** is **written on something**,
Like a **message inside of a book**.
To **transcribe** is to **write a copy**,
Like a phony check (if you're a crook).

Now you:

_____

_____

_____

_____

_____

SOPH
Knowledge, Wise

Sophistication
("Suh-FIS-tih-KAY-shun")

Philosophical
("Fil-uh-SOF-ih-kul")

Sophist
("SOF-ist")

Sophism
("SOF-iz-em")

If you have **manners** and **poise**,
And you reek of **education**,
That implies that you're **wise**,
And you possess **sophistication**.

If you're **philosophical**,
You're in a **search for truth**.
You **dig for deeper meaning**—
A **wise** kind of sleuth.

And here it takes a turn. Pay attention, you'll learn.
A **sophist** is a big **deceiver**
(Careful there, you young believer).
He **crafts his arguments to fool**.
Any class for that in school?
Sophisms are **arguments** the **sophist** designs.
To win a fight, a **sophist** crosses all kinds of lines.

This once cracks me up:
You know what **sophomore** means?
Broken down, it means Wise Moron.
Does that offend any teens?

Now you:

_____

_____

_____

_____

_____

SPAR, SPERS
Scatter

Aspersion
("UH-sper-zhun")

Disperse
("Dis-PERSE")

Disparate
("DIS-per-it")

Disparage
("Dis-PARE-ij")

If someone casts lots of **aspersions**,
He says **nasty**, **critical things**.
He scatters the **slandery** gossip.
Aspersiony talk kinda stings.

To **disperse** is to **drive off**, to **scatter**.
The traffic cop's blow horn is loud,
So she easily frightens the people away.
She's good at **dispersing** a crowd.

Disparate simply means **different**.
It's of a **dissimilar kind**.
If you like hearing **disparate** viewpoints,
You'll have a much more open mind.

To **say lousy things about something**,
That's what it means to **disparage**.
It means to **put down** or **belittle**,
Like exes who rant about marriage.

Now you:

_____

_____

_____

_____

_____

SPEC, SPIC
Look, See

Specter
("SPEK-ter")

Retrospective
("Ret-roe-SPEK-tiv")

Circumspect
("SER-kum-spekt")

Perspicacious
("Per-spih-KAY-shus")

Spectacle and **specimen**, **specific** and **inspector**
(Watch out for that last one
'Cause he has a lie detector).
There are many words around
That have to do with **"see,"**
And if you care at all,
Then you're a language freak like me.

Now **specter**, that seems cool:
A **fearsome spirit** or a **ghost**.
Of all the **apparitions**, **specters** scare a kid the most.

And if you're **retrospective**, you **look to the past**.
Retro disco parties are a total freaking blast.

Circumspect behavior is **discreet** and **careful**, too.
You actually **give some thought**
To stupid things you shouldn't do.

If you're **perspicacious**, you are **clever** and **keen**.
I'm so **perspicacious** that I always use sunscreen,
I eat healthy cuisine, I minimize caffeine,
And I keep my contacts clean . . .
Okay, *enough* of that routine.

Now you:

_____

_____

_____

_____

_____

SUB
Under

Subliminal
("Sub-LIM-in-ul")

Subpoena
("Suh-PEE-nuh")

Subterfuge
("SUB-ter-fyooj")

Subsist
("Sub-SIST")

Subsume
("Sub-SOOM")

Subterranean
("SUB-ter-ANE-ee-in")

Subjugation
("Sub-joo-GAY-shun")

Within your unconscious lie **subliminal** thoughts.
You're **never aware** of them (so Sigmund taught).

If you're served a **subpoena**, you're **called into court**.
It means **under penalty**—hang in there, Sport.
Aren't I great with support?

You use **subterfuge** when evading a rule,
Like a **trick** or a **scheme** when you ditch out of school.

If you **live on the smallest amount**, you're **subsisting**.
You're making it, but you are **barely existing**.

Take something within or **include**—that's **subsume**.
Her tears were **subsumed** in her overall gloom.

Subterranean refers to things **underground**,
So that's where the NYC **subway** is found.

If you **conquer** and **control**, you're into **subjugation**.
I think we have a bit too much of that
Between our nations.
Why not try cohabitation?

Now you:

_____

_____

_____

_____

_____

SUPER
Above, Over

Supercilious
("SOOP-er-SIL-ee-us")

Surplus
("SER-plus")

Superfluous
("Soo-PER-floo-us")

Insuperable
("In-SOOP-er-uh-bul")

Supernova
("SOOP-er-NOE-va")

Supersede
("SOOP-er-SEED")

Supercilious means **stuck-up**.
Think you're mighty and **slick**?
That is just the *super silliest* (there's your memory trick).

A **surplus** is **more than you need**;
Superfluous means the same.
Ten's a **superfluous** number of guys
For playing a video game.

Insuperable odds **can't be overcome**,
Like one mouse against ten cats.
Then again, what if it's Mighty Mouse?
I'd like to see some of that.

A **supernova** is something **celestial**.
An **explosion** or **burst of a star**.
If you happen to be flying behind one,
Then Buddy, just say "au revoir."

Supersede is **to make obsolete**.
It means that you take the place of.
The prince **superseded** the king, which was needed.
He gave Daddy-O a big shove.

Now you:

_____

_____

_____

_____

_____

TACT, TAG, TANG

Touch

Tangent
("TAN-jent")

Tactile
("TAK-tile")

Tactful
("TAKT-ful")

Tangible
("TAN-jih-bul")

If you're **in tangent**, then you're **in contact**,
In immediate physical space,
But if you go *off* on a **tangent**, you spaz,
Then you're talking all over the place.

If it's **tactile**, I **touch it** and **hold it**,
And that's how I know something's real.
A **tactile**-type person responds to the **touch**;
She relates to the things she can **feel**.

A **nice**, **tactful** person **knows just what to say**.
If it's bad news, she can make okay.
If some guy is stupid, and that's just a fact,
She would say, "He's no genius," and that's using **tact**.

Go get me some **tangible** evidence, please,
To back up the court's accusation.
In other words, get me some facts **to hold onto**—
A **tangible**, **real** explanation.

Now you:

_____

_____

_____

_____

_____

TEN, TEND, TENT
Stretch, **Thin**

Distend
("Dis-TEND")

Extenuate
("Ex-TEN-yoo-ate")

Tendentious
("Ten-DEN-shus")

Tenuous
("TEN-yoo-us")

Attenuate
("Uh-TEN-yoo-ate")

Distending your stomach: **expanding by stretching**.
Distend it with junk food, and you'll end up retching.

Extenuate something and it's **less severe**,
Like a fault or a crime or your level of fear.
We shouldn't **extenuate** pain that we're in
'Cause all that we're doing is **calling it thin**.

A **tendentious** book has a **strong point of view**
With **bias** that's **trying to influence** you.
Tendentious assertions might **stretch all the facts**.
While **tenuous** arguments feel kind of **lax**.
That's 'cause they're **thin**, you know, **not enough fact**.
A **tenuous** thesis is easily cracked.

Attenuate something and you **make it thin**.
You **weaken** it, letting its enemies in.
That's all I have for the roots tent and tend.
Read 'em all twice and you should comprehend.

Now you:

_____

_____

_____

_____

_____

TOM
Cut

Dichotomy
("Dy-KOT-oe-mee")

Epitome
("Ee-PIT-oe-mee")

Anything ending in **ectomy**
Means the doctor is **cutting it out**.
Tonsillectomy, **appendectomy**:
Cutting something you can do without.

But what about this word: **dichotomy**?
Divided or **made up of two**.
Jekyll and Hyde were **dichotomous**.
Which of those guys was untrue?
The **epitome** of a something
Is the **most representative sample**.
All other options have been **cut away**,
Leaving this, "**the most like it**" example.

Now you:

_____

_____

_____

_____

_____

VER
True

Veracity
("Vuh-RAS-ih-tee")

Verisimilitude
("Vers-ih-MIL-ih-tood")

Veracious
("Vuh-RAY-shus")

Verily
("VARE-ih-lee")

Veracity is **truthfulness**.
You're **faithful** as the sun.
If you're noted for **veracity**,
You're **true** to everyone.

Sometimes if you're showing
Lots of **verisimilitude**,
Because you're being **truthful**,
People call you blunt or rude.

When **veracious** people talk,
The story's **accurate**, **precise**.
In a world of many liars,
Veracious is so nice.

Verily: **in truth**, **indeed**.
I did not know this word. I admit
That **verily** was one I'd never heard.
Row row row your boat
Gently down the stream
Verily verily verily verily
Truth is not a dream
(*I'm not as nutty as I seem*).

Now you:

_____

_____

_____

_____

_____

VERS, VERT
Turn

Vertigo
("VER-ti-goe")

Revert
("Ree-VERT")

Inadvertent
("In-ad-VER-tent")

Incontrovertible
("In-con-truh-VER-ti-bul")

Verticle
("VER-ti-kul")

Subvert
("Sub-VERT")

If you have **vertigo**, you're **feeling dizzy**,
While **turning around**, got yourself in a tizzy.

If you **revert** to your old habits fast,
You **go back to something you knew from the past.**
That silly old lady is wild! She **reverts**
To the Sixties when she used to wear miniskirts.

To do it **inadvertently** implies you **didn't mean it**.
Despite her lethal allergies,
By chance, she ate a peanut.
Incontrovertible evidence **cannot be overturned**.
That's the kind you want in court.
You might not end up burned.

A **verticle**'s *not* up and down.
This has a different spelling.
It's a hinge!! IT'S JUST A TURNING POINT!!
Why did I start yelling?

Someone who **subverts**
Might **overthrow** or **take by storm**.
The private school **subversion**
Was to trash the uniforms.

Now you:

_____

_____

_____

_____

_____

VOC, VOK
Call

Vocation
("Vo-KAY-shun")

Avocation
("AV-oe-KAY-shun")

Advocate
("AD-vuh-kate")

Vociferous
("Voe-SIF-er-us")

Convocation
("Kon-voe-KAY-shun")

A **vocation** is a **calling**;
It's the **job you choose** to do.
It's a **profession**. It's your **business**.
The **impulse you pursue**.

An **avocation**'s similar,
But it's more like a **hobby**.
You might collect old Bentleys
(Though that sounds a little snobby).

To **support** or **speak in favor**—
That's to **advocate**,
To **stand up for** another,
To **set a record straight**.

A **vociferous** style of talking
Is kind of **big and loud**.
It gets kind of **obnoxious**
Like a late-night, **rowdy** crowd.

And finally, a **gathering**
Might be a **convocation**.
The same kind of **assembly**
You will see at graduation.

Now you:

_____

_____

_____

_____

_____

XEN
Different, Foreign, Strange

Xenophobe
("ZEN-uh-fobe")

Xenophile
("ZEN-uh-file")

Xenogenesis
("Zen-uh-JEN-uh-sis")

Xenobiotic
("Zen-uh-by-OT-ik")

Xenophobes fear foreigners.
Sometimes they even **hate 'em**.
So many hunks around the world,
But **xenophobes** won't date 'em.

On the other hand, a **xenophile**
Would **love to travel** for a while.
She **loves what's foreign, different, new**.
She'll even take a run at you.

Xenogenesis, to your dismay,
Means **you're *not* like your parents** in any way.
On the other hand, that might be good news,
But **xenogenesis** isn't something you choose.

A **substance foreign to the body**
Is called **xenobiotic**.
If you live in fear of this,
You might be called neurotic.
A **xenobiotic** chemical might be a pesticide.
Ingest enough of that crap, and your body will be fried.

Now you:

_____

_____

_____

_____

_____

Some think I'm a total nerd
To get this kind of kick from words.
But I say, come on . . . what the hell . . .
Let's try to speak *one* language well.

Index

About the Author

Jodi Fodor, MFA, is a Los Angeles–based singer/songwriter, teacher, and writer. Disney's Family.com, Americhip, and Little Tikes are among the clients for whom she has written articles, lyrics, and scripts. While helping high school students prepare for the SAT, she realized that traditional prep materials fell flat, so she created *The SAT Word Slam* to teach vocabulary with a mix of humor, sarcasm, rhyme, pop culture, celebrity mocking, teenaged angst, and mnemonics and found that the combination made the definitions practically impossible to forget. Hear some of her original songs and read more of her wry-isms at jodifodor.com.